# Business Guides on the Go

"Business Guides on the Go" presents cutting-edge insights from practice on particular topics within the fields of business, management, and finance. Written by practitioners and experts in a concise and accessible form the series provides professionals with a general understanding and a first practical approach to latest developments in business strategy, leadership, operations, HR management, innovation and technology management, marketing or digitalization. Students of business administration or management will also benefit from these practical guides for their future occupation/careers.

These Guides suit the needs of today's fast reader.

Otto Armin Smiseth

# Managing a Hospital

How to Succeed as a Clinical Leader
in the Post-Pandemic Age

 Springer

Otto Armin Smiseth
Oslo, Norway

ISSN 2731-4758          ISSN 2731-4766    (electronic)
Business Guides on the Go
ISBN 978-3-031-17613-5       ISBN 978-3-031-17611-1    (eBook)
https://doi.org/10.1007/978-3-031-17611-1

This Springer imprint is published by the registered company Springer Nature Switzerland AG.
The registered company address is: Gewerbestrasse 11, 6330 Cham, Switzerland

# Preface

This book is written for leaders at all organizational levels in hospitals. It may also be of interest to economists and politicians.

Key points in the book are that you must meet patients with empathy and respect and prove quality by showing outcome data. A hallmark of efficient leaders is ability to run good processes. Rather than working as a controller, spend most of your energy on developing better services. Set objectives for your personal contribution. Delegate as much as you can, but do it right. Recruit leaders with the right attitudes and support them in their work. Have a slim and efficient administrative staff and minimize bureaucracy

Be strong on metrics and use this to take control over the economy, instead of the economy controlling you. Improve efficiency by scaling up outpatient services, hotel capacity and by same day surgery in a hospital or in free-standing ambulatory surgical centers. See your employees when working and meet them with respect and a smile. Ultimately, your success as leader is determined by how well you interact with the employees.

Oslo, Norway                                                           Otto A. Smiseth

# Acknowledgments

These people are thanked for helpful comments in the writing process:

- Professor Emeritus Ole T. Berg. Department of Health Management and Health Economics, Institute of Health and Society, Faculty of Medicine, University of Oslo, Norway.
- Dr. Jacob Bergsland. Cardiothoracic surgeon. Past Director of Cardiothoracic Surgery and Heart Transplantation, Buffalo, New York, USA.
- Dr. Per O. Wium. Specialist in Public Health. Past Leader Health Committee, Council of Europe.
- Civil Engineer Dordi Smiseth Strand. Career as quality manager in food industry. Currently working in patient organizations, with focus on quality issues.
- Public Health Nurse Kaja P. Smiseth.

These people are thanked for valuable contributions:

- Ms Rakel Smiseth Lervold is thanked for making several of the drawings in the book.
- M.Phil. Petter Jørgensen Thorshaug is thanked for technical help.

# Key Messages

- Safety first
- Listen to employees and patients
- Take control of finance—don't let finance control you
- Be a developer, not just a controller
- Don't forget to smile

# Contents

# About the Author

**Otto Armin Smiseth** is MD, PhD, and Master of Health Administration. He is specialist in cardiology and internal medicine, with clinical training from hospitals in Norway and Canada. For 20 years, leader of several different clinical departments and divisions at Rikshospitalet and Oslo University Hospital and is immediate past Director of the Division of Cardiovascular and Pulmonary Diseases, Oslo University Hospital and University of Oslo, Norway. A key role in several hospital restructuring and merger programs. Has published several hundred international scientific articles and book chapters. Has invented and patented medical technologies. Has served as Secretary/Treasurer for the European Society of Cardiology. Has served as Chair of the European Education Committee in Cardiology and as responsible for the European Cardiology Guidelines Implementation program. Honorary Fellow of the American Society of Echocardiography. Honorary Member of several national cardiological societies. Member of the Norwegian Academy of Science and Letters. Has been Member of the Advisory Board of European Best Doctors®. From 2007 to 2020, The Personal Physician to His Majesty King Harald V of Norway. Commander of The Royal

Norwegian **Order** of **Saint Olav.** Currently, Professor Emeritus at the Medical Faculty, University of Oslo, Norway, leader of several international clinical studies and Senior Associate Editor of the European Heart Journal—Cardiovascular Imaging.

# List of Figures

# Introduction

This book is written for leaders at all organizational levels in hospitals. In addition to the intra-hospital perspective, the book discusses how the growth in hospital medicine is a financial challenge for society and calls for rethinking of the hospital organization. Therefore, the book hopefully also will be of interest to economists and politicians.

Hospitals represent a fundamental value to all societies as they take care of sick people, provide competence for prevention of disease, and contribute to development of new health care technologies. Hospitals are expected to provide safe and high-quality care with good availability and should be operated in a cost-efficient manner. This should be done with empathy and dignity and with sensitivity for the needs of patients and their families. There should be an atmosphere which inspires hope to the patients.

*Safety, quality, and empathy are core values for a hospital.*

Hospitals should incorporate feedback and opinions from patients and patient organizations and use this to improve services.

To provide best possible care, it is essential that hospitals have a healthy economy which allows adequate staffing and use of novel evidence-based medicines. A lesson from the Covid-19 pandemic is that society and hospitals should make plans for managing major crises, not only due to dangerous microorganisms, but other relevant scenarios should also be considered.

When reading this book, it is important to be aware that the organizational structure in hospitals varies widely between countries and also within countries. The names of the different organizational units used in this book are *division* as the highest organizational level and *departments* and then *sections* at lower levels. In some countries, the names are used differently, and with *department* as highest level. For simplicity and consistency, this book is written with only one organizational structure, which is with *division* at the top, and the division head reports to the CEO (Hospital Director).

Most of the book was written in late evenings and weekends when I was leader of a large and busy clinical unit. Parts of the book are like a report directly from my life as clinical leader, whereas other parts are written after I stepped down as leader and give a perspective on hospitals from the outside.

This is a hands-on book, and most of my recommendations have been tested by myself and are feasible to implement in most hospital organizations. There is no magic in obtaining excellent results, it is essentially a matter of attitude, understanding of best practice management and involving the employees. By following the principles explained in this book, there is a good chance that you will be successful as clinical leader.

# 1

# Safety First

**Abstract** In hospitals, the Director (CEO) is responsible for patient safety in the entire hospital. Similarly, the clinical leaders are responsible for patient safety within their respective units. Patient safety is about good systems and clear responsibilities throughout the organization. Furthermore, there is need for a formal structure to support the clinical leaders in their work with patient safety. This includes a director of patient safety centrally in the hospital and patient safety officers in each large clinical unit. Furthermore, there must be a patient safety committee which reviews all serious events and takes initiatives to improve clinical practice. In most cases, medical errors are due to system weaknesses, and therefore the leaders are as responsible as employees when medical errors happen.

A key element in patient safety is that clinical leaders should have continuous access to health outcome data and complication numbers in order to change clinical routines when needed. The safety work should be integrated into the daily clinical practice at the small and large units. The clinical leaders should be active and visible as role models in their work with patient safety.

© The Author(s), under exclusive license to Springer Nature Switzerland AG 2023
O. A. Smiseth, *Managing a Hospital*, Business Guides on the Go,
https://doi.org/10.1007/978-3-031-17611-1_1

The potential for improvement of patient safety in hospitals is large, as indicated by a report from researchers at Johns Hopkins University School of Medicine showing that medical errors is one of the leading causes of death in the USA (Makary & Daniel, 2016.)

> Medical errors is the third leading cause of death in the U.S. after heart disease and cancer. From Makary and Daniel, BMJ 2016.

In a hospital, the director (CEO) is responsible for patient safety in the entire hospital, and the clinical leaders are responsible for patient safety within their respective units.

To support the work with patient safety, hospitals have an organizational structure at the director level and within the clinical units to help clinical leaders and employees in their work with patient safety.

At the top of the organization, there is a *director of patient safety* who reports to the hospital director. The role of the patient safety director and her staff is to supervise and help the clinical units to build and run their own patient safety program. There is often a combined position as director of patient safety and quality.

> Director of patient safety is one of the most important positions in a hospital and here you need a respected clinical doctor to get the authority needed.

In the larger clinical units, which are named divisions, there is also need for an organizational structure which provides support to leaders in their work with patient safety and quality. This should include a *patient safety officer* who reports to the division head, and also provides support to other clinical leaders. Importantly, the clinical leaders are personally responsible for clinical result in their unit, and this responsibility cannot be delegated to the patient safety officer. The principles of delegation are discussed in more detail in Sect. 10.3. Furthermore, there is need for a *patient safety committee* with a senior medical doctor as leader. A group of employees from different health professions are appointed as members of the patient safety committee.

The leader of the patient safety committee reports to the division head. All serious events are reviewed. Based on events, one seeks to improve medical practice. To verify that this really happens, the patient safety officer should monitor and report back regularly to the safety committee regarding implementation of their decisions. Have a *to-do list*, visible in the clinical units, where each decision is listed, and keep it on the list until the decision is implemented.

The patient safety officer should be proactive and in collaboration with the clinical leaders, establish systems for implementation of safety routines. If routines are not in place, there is always a risk that errors will be repeated. One should apply the principles of the *quality circle* with the four key elements; plan, implement, check, and correct. It is recommended that each clinical unit is revised regularly to make sure that safety routines are in place.

> It is not sufficient with adjustment of routines after single incidents. Be systematic, and integrate patient safety discussions into the daily meetings with employees.

If the work with patient safety is random and only based on making corrections after errors, it is difficult to achieve the level of safety which is expected and needed in hospitals. There are good examples that systematic work leads to improvement. One example is from hospitals which have implemented a program named *safe surgery*. This is a routine where all members of a surgical team get together immediately before start of the operation, and go through a checklist. It takes only a few minutes for each surgical procedure and is an efficient method to prevent errors.

The patient safety officer should learn from best practice hospitals, and may also learn from industries such as airlines and others with high risk of severe incidents.

To make the patient safety work efficient, patient safety should be a topic in meetings where clinical decisions are taken. Safety work should not be disconnected from the daily routine, it must be integrated into the daily discussions among employees who work directly with patients.

It is an obligation for the hospital director to have uninterrupted and up to date insight into patient safety, and to take action when needed.

The hospital director, who is responsible for patient safety in the entire hospital, must be regularly updated on status of patient safety. It is not enough to organize annual conferences or have discussions in the hospital board about the importance of patient safety. The real safety work happens out in the clinical units, and the hospital director must always be up to date on the status. If his is not done properly, things may go wrong not only for patients, but also for the hospital director, as illustrated in the next chapter.

Medical errors are most often due to system failure, and therefore the leader is as responsible as an employee who has made a mistake.

When a doctor or a nurse makes a serious mistake, it is most often a problem with the systems. This is illustrated by the following case which happened in a hospital where I was working.

There was an incident where a nurse injected wrong medicine in a dangerous dose, but fortunately the patient got no permanent damage. In this case, the system more than the nurse was to blame as there was no control routine at the point of care. After this and a few other similar cases, the hospital made a rule that prior to every injection of medicine, there should be a double control where a second nurse checks the medicine and the dose prior to injection.

A frequent complaint from patient and family after medical errors is that they did not get adequate information about what happened.

It is important to establish a culture which favors openness about medical errors. The focus, however, should not be on blaming and punishing the involved employee, but to find ways to learn from the error and prevent their recurrence. Importantly, the patient and when relevant, the patient's family, should be informed immediately when a medical error has caused patient injury. Offer the patient and family to come back at a later stage for additional information since it is difficult to grasp all details in the acute or early phase after a tragic incident. Furthermore, always inform the patient about their right to file a complaint about the medical error to the local health authorities.

> The hospital should favor a culture of openness about medical errors. The focus should be on learning from the error rather than blaming the involved employee.

Furthermore, it is essential that details about the incidence is documented in the hospital file of the patient. In cases when the hospital is sued for medical error, a frequent weakness from the hospital point of view is that the involved doctors have documented too little about what actually happened, and this weakens the case for the hospital. A frequently missing documentation is verification that the patient was informed about potential complications and risks prior to the procedure. In some countries, it is tradition that the patient signs documents with information about complications and risk prior to the surgery or other procedures. This is a good practice which should be used more widely.

> Do not limit yourself to be a passive receiver of complication reports—actively support the employees with their safety programmes!

## 1.1 Patient Safety rounds

**Show Real Interest in Patient Safety by Frequent Safety Rounds** These are rounds by the division head or department head, who visits and meets with one clinical unit at a time. In the following, the examples are given for the division head doing these rounds. Here the division head gets an opportunity to talk with the employees "on the floor" about safety issues. The objective is to come up with measures which can improve safety. Importantly, these rounds demonstrate for the employees that you as a leader care about patient safety. The patient safety officer participates in the safety rounds and acts as secretary for the rounds, taking notes and helping the division head to follow up on matters which need to be taken care of.

As leader you must show visible involvement in the patient safety programme.

The way I do it, the safety rounds start with myself as division head, meeting with a small group of three to four employees. These are people who work close to patients. I start with reviewing briefly what was achieved since the last meeting. Then the employees present what is their most important issues to discuss with regard to patient safety. Based upon what is presented and discussed, a short list is made with no more than three action points.

Then the employees leave the room, and the local leaders enter the room. The list of action points is presented and final decisions can be made. This meeting which I ideally have once a week must be time efficient. The way I do it, the meeting lasts 40 minutes, 30 minutes with the employees and 10 minutes with the leaders. These are great meetings because the top leader gets a chance to meet the people working close to the patients, and important decisions regarding safety can be taken with little bureaucracy.

I have also tried having one patient representative joining me on these rounds, and it has been successful. I remember in particular one, let us call him Robert, who was the kind of person who was critical in a constructive way and always friendly. We trusted him and showed him also the "dirty laundry" of our hospital. When Robert proposed changes, like getting more modern equipment or adding nurses where there was a shortage, his opinions were always considered when we made decisions regarding patient safety issues.

Figure 1.1 shows key points for what is expected from clinical leaders with regard to patient safety.

## 1.2    Safety at Point of Care: Safety Cross

A safety cross is a collection of incidents in a one-month calendar where red color means there was an incident that day and green means things were fine (Fig. 1.2). It may be used in the wards and in other units. As an example, the nurses may decide one month to record the number of patient falls. In the calendar, the nurses each morning take the couple of

> **The leader's role in patient safety – This is the minimum**
> • Meet regularly with your patient safety officer
>   and patient safety committee
> • Make safety rounds to clinical units
> • Have updated plans for health crisis (Covid-19 lesson)
> • Provide annual reports of complications

**Fig. 1.1** Expectations to clinical leaders in their work with patient safety. Copyright: Otto A. Smiseth

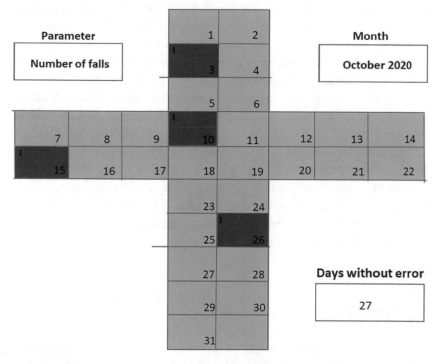

**Fig. 1.2** Safety cross. Green means no incident and red that an incident occurred that day. Number of incidents are indicated in the upper left corners. Copyright: Otto A. Smiseth

minutes to record number of falls. This can be done on a board or on an electronic sheet displayed to the entire team. This way you get daily focus on errors. It can be done for several types of errors simultaneously or with focus on just one type of error each month. Monthly results are displayed for leaders, staff, and visitors and are a good background for discussing improvement in safety.

**Patients Should Not Only Be Safe, But Also Feel Safe** Prior to arrival in the hospital, the patient should be informed about what will happen, which tests are planned and how they will be done. The patient should have the name of their nurse and doctor and whom to contact prior to the hospital visit. This is all about feeling safe. Furthermore, they should know whom to contact after discharge in case they need additional information or help. Lessons from the Covid-19 Pandemic During the Covid-19 pandemic, most countries experienced too low hospital bed capacity, in particular intensive care beds, and there was shortage of ventilators and personal protective equipment. There was also severe shortage of doctors and nurses, in particular intensive care nurses. This calls for new systems for mobilizing reserve personnel in such situations, which is discussed in Sect. 5.26. There is also need for rethinking hospital infrastructure, and if changes are needed to allow isolation of infected patients while maintaining capacity for other patients. It is not acceptable that patients with potentially deadly diseases, such as cancer and heart disease, have several months of delay in treatment. There are many lessons from the Covid-19 pandemic, and these need to be addressed, and should lead to better preparation for a next crisis.

# Reference

Makary, M. A., & Daniel, M. (2016, May 3). Medical error-the third leading cause of death in the US. *BMJ, 353*, i2139. https://doi.org/10.1136/bmj.i2139.

# 2

# Prove Quality

**Abstract** From a patient perspective, quality is about the total experience with a hospital, and includes not only medical quality, but also safety, empathy, service attitude, timeliness of care and information. This chapter addresses medical quality, and other quality aspects are discussed in other chapters.

Every hospital should give patients access to quality data on the hospital website, so that patients can use this information when deciding which hospital to use. Indicators of medical quality are categorized into three types; structure, process, and outcome indicators. Structure includes factors such as number of beds, if there are specialized units in oncology, neurology, etc. Process indicators refer to documents and training standards. What matters the most for patients is data on health outcome, which is about change in health and complications to different treatments. Surprisingly few hospitals provide data on health outcome. There is a trend in the USA that outcome data is a requirement to get contract with health providers.

Every clinical leader must be continuously updated on outcomes, including complication rates in their own unit, and must take action whenever needed. The hospital director must have access to outcome data for the entire hospital and how each clinical unit is performing.

O. A. Smiseth, *Managing a Hospital*, Business Guides on the Go,
https://doi.org/10.1007/978-3-031-17611-1_2

From a patient perspective, quality is not only about medical competence. It is the total experience with the hospital that matters, and in addition to medical quality, this includes safety, empathy, service attitude, timeliness of care and information. This chapter discusses *medical quality*. Other aspects of quality are addressed in different chapters in this book.

Data on hospital quality is of interest not only to patients and referring physicians when they select hospitals, but is also important for insurance companies and governments when deciding hospitals they want to contract. In the USA, there is a system where Medicare-certified hospitals present quality data on their website. This is illustrated in Fig. 2.1.

Quality indicators can be classified into three types; *structure, process, and outcome indicators.* Indicators of structure may include number of beds within each medical specialty, patient volume for specific diseases, if there are specialized units for oncology, cardiology, neurology and others, and number of medical specialists, etc. Process indicators include factors such as routines for training and certifying employees, standards of medical procedures, adherence to medical guidelines, etc. The indicators listed above are fine, but do not replace the need for indicators of health outcome. Every hospital can make nice documents about how to ensure

**Fig. 2.1** Hospital Compare has information about the quality of care at over 4.000 Medicare-certified hospitals in the US. This information helps patients and referring physicians when selecting hospital

safety and quality, but what matters for the patients is how things are in the real world. Hospitals often have large numbers of procedures in the digital quality system, but no data about what happened to the patients.

## 2.1  Outcome Data Is the Most Important

Health outcome is defined as the change in health after treatment. The most important outcomes are change in health status measured objectively or as expressed by the patients, frequency of severe complications, and mortality during the hospital stay and long term (e.g., 30 days). Which outcome measures to use are often defined by national organizations.

Importantly, assessment of medical quality can be used by hospital employees to improve their own performance. One example is complication data for surgical procedures and interventions. The individual data do not need to be communicated to everybody in the department, but each surgeon should know how he performs compared to the other surgeons in the same department, and his leader should have access to the data. Furthermore, the hospital director who is responsible for everything in the hospital should have continuous insight into outcome data.

**When Quality Systems Fail: A Real-Life Case**  In one of the European hospitals, there was a severe case that was presented in the prime-time TV news. Five patients who became physically disabled due to complications during orthopedic surgery, were protesting against the hospital director by rallying outside the hospital. They were all operated by the same surgeon. The list of complications from this surgeon was long, and these patients were protesting because the hospital director allowed this to happen. One of the patients, who was interviewed on television, was crying when she explained how the complication affected her life. Thereafter, the hospital director was interviewed on television, but she seemed paralyzed and was not able to give good answers.

The true story was that the hospital director had no idea that this surgeon had high complication rates since there was no metrics on outcome in the hospital. This was a bad case for everybody, first of all for the patients, but also for the hospital and for the surgeon. If there had been a system in place for reporting of outcome data, his superior would have picked this up, and appropriate action could have been taken.

This case illustrates the obligation of clinical leaders and the hospital director to be up to date on outcome data in their hospital, and the need to take action when results are not according to good quality standards.

Every hospital director has improvement of quality as one of the key strategic objectives. Heroic statements like *in this hospital we put medical quality first* are not uncommon. Unfortunately, you rarely find hospitals with quality programs at the level you find in many industries.

Some countries have centralized systems at government level where hospitals have to send reports when serious events happen. This may be useful for statistics, but has limited effects on patient safety and quality. As part of the system, government bureaucrats may initiate investigations with the objective to find the reason for the medical errors, and new operative procedures are made to reduce the risk that the same error will be repeated. This system which typically involves several layers of bureaucrats, takes responsibility away from the clinical leaders, and therefore is highly inefficient. Ensuring quality and patient safety is a responsibility of the leaders inside the hospital, and this should include reporting outcome data.

Some hospitals report outcome data to national or local registries, and annual reports are generated. If patients could get access to these data in a user-friendly way, the registries would be an important step in the right direction. Hospitals which report data to such registries, should extract relevant outcome data and present these on the hospital website.

*Hospital leaders should be prepared for a rapid development towards systems where payment for all hospital services isis linked to metrics on quality. A majority of Medicare fee for service payments already have a link to quality.*

In the USA, Medicare payments are already tied to quality, and the expectation is that similar models will be common in other countries in the near future. Therefore, hospitals need to establish metrics on quality in order to be competitive.

Naturally, patients who are scheduled for surgery or other therapies may have concerns about quality and safety. The most important is to know how likely it is that your health will improve and the risk of complications. Surprisingly few patients actively request to see such data. This may reflect that people traditionally believe that most hospitals are just fine, or they may think that asking for this may give resentment in the hospital. Some patients do, however, ask for outcome data, but often get no answer since there are limited data available and often nothing on the hospital websites. When you arrive in the hospital, your doctor and nurse usually touch on the issue of complications and risks, but when you already are in the process of starting treatment, it is for most people very difficult to turn down the offer, in particular if you have waited for a long time to get access.

In some countries, there is increasing demand from patients to see outcome data, and hospitals are slowly adapting to this new environment. Some hospitals, however, are excellent in this regard and present comprehensive quality data, including outcome data on their website.

In the heart and lung surgery departments in the divisions I have been leading, I was fortunate to have *surgeons* who provided continuous, fresh outcome data (Svennevig, 2021). At the end of each month, the leaders receive data on mortality and complications for different categories of patients. By having fresh data every month, the leaders are always up to date on the level of medical quality in the surgical units. They also receive 30 days mortality numbers which are very important for understanding the longer-term outcome. At the end of the year, they compare results in their own units with those from other countries who report similar data.

## 2.2   Volume Data Reflect Quality

Training and experience can be expressed in terms of "volume data," which are numbers for specific surgeries or other procedures done annually at the hospital. The term *volume/quality* implies that high volume is better than low volume for training and quality.

In the USA, there are annual reports, based on the opinion of several thousand doctors, which rank hospitals and medical specialties. This is much better than nothing, but many of the hospitals on the list have only limited quality data on their website. In the absence of quality data, the patient usually leaves it to their referring physician to select hospital. In the absence of outcome data at the hospital which is selected, this is a rather weak system.

In several countries with universal healthcare coverage, there is essentially monopoly, and therefore the patients have limited choice of hospital and need to accept whatever standard they get. This is not accepted by all patients, and therefore "medical tourism" is a growing business where patients pay themselves to be treated at good hospitals in other countries.

## 2.3   Present Complication Data, But Do It Right

The most essential complication data are mortality and frequency of severe, disabling complications. Not to scare the patients away from your hospital, the presentation should include reference to what is expected complication rates at other good hospitals.

One should avoid too much focus on complication rates without taking patient complexity into account. If not done properly, it may act as a negative incentive for surgeons to operate the sickest patients who need surgery the most, but also are associated with more complications than most other patients.

A hallmark of great surgeons is that they undertake the most demanding surgery, even when the likelihood that the patient will survive is not the highest, but the surgery is their only chance. These surgeons have courage to fail, and they are needed to rescue the sickest of the sick.

Making surgeons personally accountable for their complication statistics can have the unwanted effects that they feel punished for operating the sickest patients. Instead, publish complication statistics for the entire surgical unit and accompanied by appropriate text which describes the complexities of the patients that are operated.

*Avoid making the surgeons personally accountable for their complication statis-*
*ticssince the best surgeons can be scared from helping the sickest patients.*

Another negative consequence of making surgeons personally accountable for their complication statistics is that training of young surgeons
may suffer, since training can slightly increase complication risk. Training
of new surgeons is of course in the best interest of patients.

In different hospitals, systems for recording and reporting outcome
data have variable quality, and therefore support is needed to secure standardization of systems. This may be done by national health authorities
or dedicated agencies who perform audits, where experts on the systems
visit hospitals and exert controller function and provide support.

## 2.4   Document Adherence to Guidelines

When outcome data are not available, an alternative is to report data on
adherence to clinical practice guidelines. As an example, if a hospital
treats only 40% of patients with multiple sclerosis according to guidelines, it is important for the patients to know. Some patients may want to
find a different hospital, one where all patients receive the best available
medicine. Another example, if a hospital which operates patients with
lung cancer does not screen for metastasis with novel imaging technologies as recommended in current guidelines, the patient should know. It
can be a disaster for the patient if only the primary lung cancer is removed,
while a deadly metastasis is not detected and taken care of. Some of the
recommendations in the national or international practice guidelines
imply high end, expensive technologies, and therefore finances often
limit full implementation of recommendations in guidelines. The
patients, however, have a right to know if the hospital provides the best
available treatment for their disease, and might want to pick a different
hospital if they are not satisfied.

*The patient has a right to know if a hospital offers best available therapy.*

Hospitals that want to present quality data in terms of adherence to guidelines can do this with limited efforts if they have modern digital patient records. They can show percentage of patients who receive guidelines-based medicine for specific conditions at hospital discharge. Even if this is done for only a limited number of diseases, it shows that the hospital has focus on practicing evidence-based medicine. It is useful in particular for diseases where health outcome is not easily measured.

## 2.5    What About Quality Data in Psychiatry?

In psychiatry there are less developed quality measures than in somatic medicine. This reflects the complexity of services within mental health care and limited standardization of quality measures. This should, however, not be used as an excuse for not presenting quality data on the hospital website. Similar to somatic medicine, quality of health services in psychiatry is measured with basis in structure, process, and outcome.

## 2.6    Help Patients Who Want a Second Opinion

If a patient wants referral to another hospital for whatever reason, you should help the patient with writing the letters needed. The same applies to patients who want referral for a second opinion, you should facilitate it. I was for several years member of the Medical Advisory Board for Best Doctors, which is a company that helps patients to get the best available medical service and second opinions. This is a global company which has a wide network of physicians who are selected as best in their field by other leading doctors. The company was founded many years ago by Harvard Medical School professors in response to an increasing number of requests for second opinion and medical advice from colleagues. My learning from working with this company, was that medical diagnosis were frequently not entirely correct and sometimes completely wrong. Therefore, it is reasonable that patients request second opinions. Importantly, a second opinion should be considered a learning opportunity for the local doctor and should not be considered a complaint.

## 2.7   The Importance of Respecting Patient Preferences

Patient's trust in physician and hospital is fundamental to the care process, and respect for the individual patient's right to make their own health care decisions is essential (Fig. 2.2). Some countries, however, have systems which enforces patients to use hospitals owned by the government, and the patient is given limited or no freedom to choose hospital and physician. In some of these countries there are no hospital performance data in terms of health outcome, which makes these systems even worse for the patients. Other countries have systems where the patients can select hospital and physician. The latter model of course is what most patients prefer. Governments should ensure that all inhabitants get access to state-of-the-art healthcare, and autonomy of patients to select hospital and physician should be respected.

---

**Always the patient first**

✓ Show quality data on the hospital website, to help patients decide which hospital to choose.

✓ Be supportive when a patient wants referral for a second opinion.

✓ Meet regularly with patient organizations, and involve them in development of the hospital services.

---

**Fig. 2.2**  Always the patient first. Copyright: Otto A. Smiseth

## 2.8 Physicians Doing Research Is a Quality Marker

It is important for leaders in university hospitals and in some other hospitals, to understand that research is a core activity which should be supported. Doctors and other health professionals who conduct research often have international networks which can benefit the patients.

Research also includes collaboration with industry, which usually plays a key role in developing new drugs and technologies. Therefore, it is important that leaders in hospitals support industry collaboration. This is needed for progress in medical technology, which ultimately determines much of the quality when it comes to novel therapies.

## 2.9 Support Employees Who Want External Training

Make sure that your employees get access to teaching courses and attend medical conventions where recent innovations are presented. It is also important that physicians and nurses have part of their training at other places than in their own hospital. They should not just travel and *see*, they should be encouraged to *work* in a top center at another institution.

## Reference

Svennevig, J. L. (2021, Apr 23). Requirement for quality control of surgery. *Tidsskr Nor Laegeforen, 141*(7).

# 3

# Show Empathy

**Abstract** Empathy is a core value of all hospitals, and is the sine qua non of good leadership. Empathy is about considering other people's feelings, and is an essential part of social intelligence. Empathy cannot be compensated by superb academic degrees or technical skills.

## 3.1 Empathy Is a Core Value for Hospitals

In hospitals and other knowledge organizations, social intelligence is the sine qua non of good leadership, and empathy is an essential part of *social intelligence*. Empathy is about considering other people's feelings. Great mathematical type intelligence, superb technical skills or a master's degree in management from the best universities cannot compensate for insufficient empathy.

Empathy is something fundamental to a personality, and we all appreciate talking to people who show empathy. We see it in their facial expression, in the way they talk, how they listen and ask questions and how they adapt to your emotional rhythm in a given situation. When you are a leader, empathy becomes increasingly important.

People with empathy can more easily resolve conflicts since they better understand how their opponents feel. Rather than seeing the matter only from their own point of view, they can feel how it is to be in the shoes of their opponents.

The more I have been working with people in different organizations, the more I also appreciate *kindness*. My first boss was Professor Ole D. Mjøs. He was exceptionally successful both in medical research and politics, and for a long time, he was chair of the Nobel Peace Prize Committee. What made him successful was not only ambition and personal drive, but even more his empathy and kindness.

## 3.2   Be Aware of Your Behavior

In 1995 Daniel Goleman published the book *Emotional Intelligence (Goleman,* 1995), and it became extremely popular. The concept of emotional intelligence has ever since been fundamental to understanding what good management is about.

An important component of emotional intelligence is *self-awareness,* which is about understanding how your behavior and personality impacts other people. I have seen leaders who are great people and even are empathic, but their behavior creates an atmosphere of distance. Others who are actually very nice and friendly people have an appearance of arrogance which nobody dear to tell them, which reduces their potential as leaders. Not uncommonly, some leaders do most of the talking themselves and rarely listen, which also reduces their potential to be efficient leaders. Examples are numerous of how suboptimal behavior and too little self-awareness reduces the potential of talented people to become good leaders.

> *The good news is that behavior can be modified, but only if you became aware of the problem yourself.*

When you have become a top leader, there are not that many people who dare to give you feedback about your behavior. Sometimes your family can give you feedback which is great, although it can ruin a pleasant family dinner. In ancient Rome, victorious military commanders, when riding through cheering crowds, would have a trusted slave behind them to whisper continuously in their ear "*Memento Mori*" ("remember you are mortal"), to bring their ego feeling down to the ground. It is challenging to give feedback that touches people's personality and ego, but when it is done confidentially and by someone they trust, it is of good help.

*Self-regulation* is another important component of emotional intelligence and is about self-control and avoiding disruptive behavior. Leaders with good self-regulation are able to control their emotions and reactions when interacting with other people. Social intelligence, including self-regulation, is fundamental to a personality and to a large extent, is determined by genes and social experience in early life. In spite of that, social intelligence can be modified and improved by training.

## 3.3 The Hospital Is Not a Repair Shop: It Is All About Empathy

Patients, accompanying relatives and care partners should be met as human beings with feelings, sometimes in emotional imbalance and we should accept and not blame them for whatever they may say about the hospital. The way the doctor and the nurse meet the patients is important for their health. It is also important for the reputation of the hospital. A professional nurse or doctor should always show empathy and understanding and should facilitate an open dialogue with patient and relatives.

## Reference

Goleman, D. (1995). *Emotional intelligence*. Bantam Books.

# 4

# Reduce the Administrative Burden

**Abstract** The hierarchical organization is common in hospitals. This model has vertical lines of command between units. At the top is the hospital director (CEO), and the units below have different names in different hospitals. An alternative is the matrix organization, with horizontal lines crossing the vertical lines of command. Matrix organization facilitates coordination between departments.

In addition to health professionals, hospitals have support staff, which includes secretarial services and important technical functions. Furthermore, there is an *administrative staff,* which includes a finance manager, an HR manager, and a patient safety officer. An efficient administrative staff takes care of a large part of the administrative workload. With an efficient administrative staff, the clinical leader can free up time to be leader, get some protected time and avoid spending most of the time on administrative routines.

Make sure your agenda is well structured and focused on the essentials. Then you can free up substantial protected time to your own disposal.

In addition to the standard administrative meetings, it is recommended to meet each subordinate leader and key administrative staff weekly in brief one-on-one meetings. Furthermore, a weekly "walking and smiling" round to most of your clinical units is recommended.

# 4.1    Organization: Chain of Command

Hospitals, similar to other types of businesses, are organized with a CEO (chief executive officer) on top. In some countries, the title of the CEO is Hospital Director. The next level is divisions, and each division includes several departments. Furthermore, departments often have specialized units for diagnostics and treatment, and there are wards where the beds are located. These subunits within departments have different names, but in this book, they are referred to as sections. There may also be smaller units below the sections.

In some hospitals, organizational levels are given numbers. The hospital director is level 1, divisions are level 2, departments are level 3, and sections are level 4. When there are units below sections, they are level 5. When the department head reports directly to the hospital director, the departments are level 2, etc.

A division usually takes care of diseases which are related. An example is division of oncology which typically has departments of medical oncology, surgical oncology, radiation therapy and there may also be other departments. In smaller hospitals, there are usually no divisions, and the department heads report directly to the hospital director. The organizational model which is discussed in this book is with divisions, departments, and sections. Most of what is written about division heads also applies to department heads, and to heads of the smaller units. In several places, it is referred to doctors and nurses, but the principles discussed in this book applies to other health workers as well.

Figure 4.1 shows an organizational structure which is common in hospitals, and is named a hierarchical organization. This is a "vertical" type of organization that originates from the military. The figure illustrates the chain of command, and when using the military as model, the red lines show where orders can be passed between different levels in the organization. The person with the highest level of command is the hospital director (CEO). Orders can be passed from the hospital director to the division head, who can either execute the order himself or pass it down to the department head. The hospital director reports to the chair of the

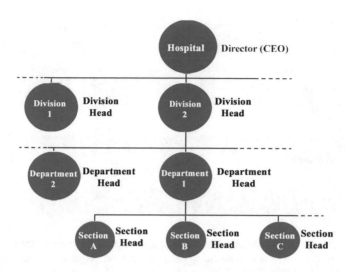

**Fig. 4.1** Hierarchical organization in a hospital. The chain of command is indicated by red lines. In some hospitals, there are no divisions, and the department heads report directly to the hospital director. Copyright: Otto A. Smiseth

hospital board. This is what is named *line management*, which means you follow the administrative lines.

Another type of organization is matrix organization which is illustrated in Fig. 4.2. In a matrix organization, there are horizontal lines of responsibility crossing the vertical lines of command. The example in Fig. 4.2 is from a cardiovascular division. The two horizontal lines of responsibility represent the departments of Outpatient Care and Secretarial Services, which provide services to all the other departments. Unless the departments are very large, this is a more efficient solution than establishing separate outpatient units and secretarial units within each clinical department.

A third type is the flat organization, also known as horizontal organization. This is an organizational structure where all employees are in principle on the same level. The idea behind flat organizations is that well-trained workers will be more productive when they are more directly involved in the decision-making process, rather than being supervised by layers of management. This structure is generally possible only in smaller organizations or in small units within larger organizations.

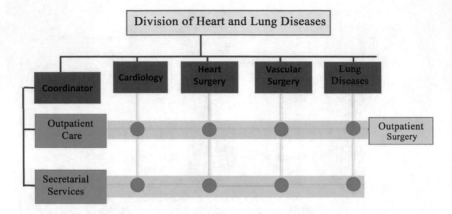

**Fig. 4.2** Matrix organization: The read and dark blue boxes are departments. In addition to the vertical command lines, there are horizontal lines of responsibility. Copyright: Otto A. Smiseth

Hospitals are often like big enterprises with several hundred or even several thousand employees. Therefore, it is critical that the organizational structure is well understood and that leaders and employees act according to their authority and responsibility.

Every leader and employee need to understand how the chain of command works. A leader can instruct only those directly below them in the chain of command and receive orders only from those directly above them. To

At each level in the organization, a leader is responsible for everything within his own unit, and the hospital director is responsible for everything in the entire hospital.

use the organization in Fig. 4.1 as an example, the head of Department 1 can instruct section heads A, B, and C. The head of Department 2, however, cannot instruct the heads of sections A, B, and C since they are not in the same line of command. The hospital director can instruct the division heads, but not the department heads or section heads because that would be incorrect with respect to the authority of the division and department heads.

There are many different definitions of what a leader is, and there is no universal consensus. The title of the leader also varies between hospitals, and even inside the same hospital. In addition to leader, it is common to use titles such as chair, head, chief, boss, or director. It is not critical which title is used, but for a hospital it may sound better that you lead, implying that people are expected to follow you, than being chief, which is more associated with giving orders. In this book, the terms *leader* and sometimes *head* are used for leaders who are in the line of command. Manager is used for people leading groups such as finance and HR who are not in the line of command. Sometimes the term *boss* is used, which is a more informal title with the advantage that everybody understand that this is the person in charge.

Titles like medical director or nurse director can be a bit confusing since in most cases people with these titles are not leaders. The title program director is sometimes used, and this is usually a medical doctor or nurse who is responsible for providing services to a defined patient group. They provide services across the different units, but are not leaders as defined above with responsibility for the total result, including medical services, economy, manpower and EHS.

In addition to leaders, there are coordinators who, as the title indicates, coordinate activities on behalf of the leaders.

Most hospitals have team-based management. In divisions there is a management group which consists of the division head and all the department heads. Furthermore, the HR manager and the finance manager usually are members of the management group. The departments may also have a management group consisting of the department head and all the section heads.

The definition and authority of a leader should be clear to everybody. It is fundamental for successful organizations that there is only one leader for each of the units. This is more important in hospitals than in most other types of companies or businesses since decisions made in hospitals are about life and death.

I was surprised to find out recently that in some European countries, hospitals still have separate lines of command for doctors and nurses, all the way up to the hospital director. This type of old-fashioned, non-functional management structure apparently is difficult to get rid of. In my home country which is Norway, the Parliament passed a law about

20 years ago which made it obligatory with only one leader at all organizational levels in hospitals. Furthermore, it was decided that all leaders should be professionally neutral. In my view, this was a needed and good change. This means, if a department head is a medical doctor, she is chief of all personnel, including nurses and secretaries. Similarly, if the department head is a nurse, she is chief also of the medical doctors. In practice, however, it is often preferable to have local leaders who are experts in the respective activities within the unit they are leading.

> By all means try to avoid dual leadership with separate organizational lines for doctors and nurses. Such a structure makes it unclear who is responsible for the patient and is highly inefficient.

## 4.2 Organization: Hospital Support Staff

In addition to doctors, nurses, and other health professionals, every hospital has a support staff. They take care of information technology, maintenance, cleaning, patient transport and other basic functions. Within the clinical units, the secretaries provide important support to doctors and nurses. Furthermore, there is a group of support staff working with finance, human resources and patient safety, and in the following, they are referred to as *administrative staff*. Figure 4.3 illustrates staff at different levels in a hospital.

In some hospitals, the administrative staff is organized centrally in the hospital as part of the hospital director's staff. In smaller hospitals, this is probably the best model to allow efficient utilization of staff capacity. With regard to management of finances, every hospital has a finance director who takes care of day-to-day financial operations and supervises financial activities, making sure they are according to local rules, regulations, and policies. The finance director and her team also take care of finance reporting, analysis, and budgeting. In hospitals with administrative staff at the division level, a finance manager takes care of these functions on behalf of the division head. There is also often a legal director in the administrative staff of the hospital director.

In larger hospitals with divisions, I recommend having key staff functions at division level and this should as a minimum include HR

**Administrative Staff**

Fig. 4.3 Example of administrative staff in a hospital. In smaller hospitals, the entire administrative staff may be at the hospital director level. Copyright: Otto A. Smiseth

manager, finance manager and patient safety officer. Furthermore, having a personal assistant for the division head and in larger departments for the department head, is very useful. To avoid the cost of additional administrative staff, departments should be served by the division staff.

In the divisions, the administrative staff takes care of daily technical issues, they have controller function for finance and employee number and they prepare budget and produce reports for the division head.

## 4.3   Make the Administrative Staff Efficient

Throughout this book, when I refer to my personal experience with making the clinic efficient, the administrative staff always played an important role. They provide the support I need to resolve the many small and big administrative issues I am facing every day as leader. Importantly, this functionality did not come without efforts, and this chapter discusses how to optimize the way the administrative staff works to provide best possible support to the leaders.

We have to acknowledge that there are important challenges with making the administrative staff efficient. Generally, the real action in a company is in the line jobs, and in a hospital, the medical doctors, nurses, and other health professionals are considered the most important since they work directly with patients.

The administrative staff often feel they are outside the real game and this is bad for their work morale. If they are not well supervised or they are too many, they may start doing things on their own initiative, and that can lead to even more frustration when they find that the clinical leaders do not want to respond to their ideas.

> The administrative staff should be respected, treated well and receive frequent feedback.

In order to make the administrative staff efficient, it is essential that they are integrated into the clinical activities so that they understand what it is all about. The only mission of the administrative staff is to support the clinical leaders, and therefore they need to have frequent contact with the leaders.

Administrative staff which are isolated from the clinical activities tend to live in their own world, and may become a burden to the organization. It is up to the division head, or department head when there is administrative staff at the department level, to prevent this from happening by defining which deliverables are expected from the administrative staff and giving them regular feedback.

> Importantly, the administrative staff should not consume a lot of the leader's time, but regular interaction between the two is needed.

I have explained in other chapters in this book, how a model with brief weakly one-on-one meetings between the division head and each one of the key administrative staff is an efficient way of securing the interaction. This should include regular meetings with the patient safety officer, the finance manager and the HR manager. These are the three critical administrative staff functions in a hospital. Since nurses represent such a large group of employees, it will often be useful with a staff person to take care of issues related to training and recruiting nurses (nurse coordinator).

When you are frustrated because your boss is demanding more than you can deliver, and your subordinates do not respond as you expect, it is always very nice to have an administrative staff to discuss with. Furthermore, having a coffee and a friendly talk with the staff makes life emotionally much better. Be careful, however, that you do not isolate yourself with the administrative staff. Seek solutions primarily through contact with your clinical leaders and employees. Furthermore, you should also expect that your boss provides constructive advice to help you out of difficult management situations. Do this by one-on-one meetings with your boss, and do not be afraid of asking for his time. These discussions are equally important for him. You will probably find that your boss has a few requests for such meetings and he will appreciate that you contact him.

> If you spend more time meeting with the administrative staff than with clinical leaders, there should come up a red flag.

How large administrative staff do you need? In a division with 500–1000 employees, two full-time positions in HR are sufficient, the HR manager and an assistant. In a division of this size, the finance manager needs a couple of assistants, including a person dedicated to controller functions. The number of administrative staff needed, however, depends upon how automated the technical administration of the hospital is. This is somewhat like modern banking, when the customer is doing most of the work, the banks can reduce the number of employees.

There are also a number of other administrative functions like taking care of IT, waiting lists, communication and internet activities, but one should avoid staffing with administrative people at the division level to take care of this. These functions are too small in a division to justify dedicated staff and should be taken care of in a slim administrative staff centrally in the hospital.

Every hospital needs someone to provide support on Environmental Health and Safety (EHS), and this can be taken care of by someone centrally in the hospital. In hospitals with large divisions, this may not be sufficient and part-time EHS positions may be needed further down in the organization.

## 4.4    Power Up Your Routines

### 4.4.1    Make the Meeting Agenda Efficient

Meetings provide real benefit as arenas for exchanging information, collaboration, and unfolding creativity. If you seriously mean that you do not like meetings, you have a significant limitation as a leader. Meetings represent arenas where you can shine as a leader and exert your leadership.

Use meetings to listen to and discuss with your subordinate leaders and employees and to show them respect for the work they are doing. People who feel they are involved and are seen by their leader will be much more motivated to help the leader.

In a Harvard Business Review article, Perlow et al. (2017) addressed the challenge of too many meetings. This included a discussion of how to free up time for "deep work" as opposed to quick superficial work. Since time is a zero-sum game, it is a problem if the meeting agenda is too extensive. It is reported that executives on average spend nearly 23 hours a week in meetings, up from less than 10 hours in the 1960s (Perlow et al., 2017), and the meetings are often poorly timed, badly run, or both.

Avoid the meeting overload, and free up time for "deep work."

Make sure your agenda is well structured and is focused on the essentials. Then you can free up substantial protected time and flexible time. Figure 4.4 is an example from a typical week in my positions as division head. I have practiced this kind of agenda as leader of divisions with 20–30 departments and sections and up to 900 employees. This figure is just one example and there is of course an unlimited number of different schedules which can work fine. The main point is to illustrate that it is feasible to free up time to do other things than the busy routine.

To attract the best people into management, it is important to make them understand that you are not spending your life running between meetings, which leaders unfortunately often communicate. There will be times when you are busy with meetings every day of the week, such as when you have to resolve unexpected financial challenges. But for

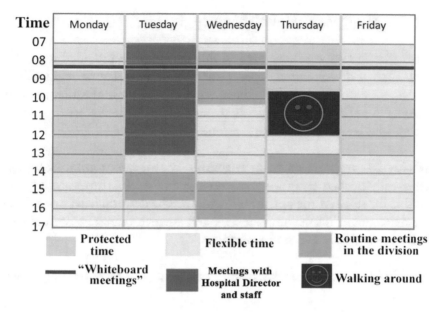

**Fig. 4.4** Example of a meeting schedule for a division head. Please note there is ample flexible time which is used for administrative meetings when needed and there is protected time. The "Walking around" is time spent with the employees as explained in Sect. 4.5 and 7.3. Copyright: Otto A. Smiseth

business as usual, which means most of the time, there is ample flexible and protected time, provided you structure your meeting schedule appropriately.

Some leaders fill all days of the week with meetings, but unless they also spend lots of time with the employees, I discourage this kind of schedule.

If there is a large project which will run for an extended period, like major reconstructions in the hospital, it may be useful to appoint a deputy for the particular project. To make this efficient, the deputy should be a trusted and competent person who can attend the meetings and make decisions on your behalf. Importantly, as with all delegation of important matters, you need to follow up that things are taken well care of.

## 4.4.2   The "Must Have" Meetings

The meeting structure suggested in this paragraph is intended for larger units such as divisions and departments. There are of course many different ways of structuring these meetings, but regardless of structure, it is essential that leaders at all units in the organization are involved, and that each leader is seen regularly and frequently by their boss.

**Weekly Management Group Meetings**  Management group meetings are usually needed every week or every second week. These meetings are needed for some of the operative decisions. The division head meets with the department heads, and the HR and finance managers are present. These are typically 1–2 hours meetings.

**Weekly Meetings in the Position Committee**  This meeting is explained in Sect. 5.11.

**Weekly Meetings with Administrative Staff**  In organizational units with their own administrative staff, it is efficient to meet with key members of the staff one at a time, every week.

The way I do this is to meet one-on-one with the patient safety officer, HR manager, finance manager and nurse coordinator (Fig. 4.5). I meet them sequentially, 10 or 15 minutes with each. Symbolically, the safety officer gets 20 minutes and meets first.

Following the one-on-one meeting with key administrative staff, I meet the entire administrative staff to give them update on recent issues and even more important, each one tells me what they will do the coming week. Although some members in the staff report to the HR manager and finance manager, and not directly to you, it gives good motivation for everyone in the staff to meet the "boss."

With a schedule as illustrated in Fig. 4.6, your most important leaders and administrative staff get a chance to talk directly with you every week. Having regular one-on-one meetings is great as the employees get all your attention, and are perfect opportunities to give and receive feedback and to build trust.

**Fig. 4.5** Division head meets with administrative staff: A brief, weekly one-on-one meeting with each one of the administrative staff is recommended. Copyright: Otto A. Smiseth

When booking meetings sequentially with no breaks, each of the attendees replaces each other automatically, and you avoid too long meetings. Furthermore, if the 10–15 meetings were spread throughout the week, it would be difficult to start and end on time, and the meetings would consume a lot more of your time.

**Monthly Report Meetings** The division head meets with the department heads, one at a time. The HR- and finance managers are also present. The objective is to update the division head on status, discuss challenges and to make operative decisions. Typically, 30 to 60 minutes meetings.

**Quarterly Report Meetings** The division head meets separately with each department. At these meetings, the department head is accompanied by all his section heads. They review the status of the department and discuss challenges. The section heads tend to like these meetings since they get a chance to meet face to face the division head. HR- and finance managers and safety officer are present. Typically, these are one-hour meetings.

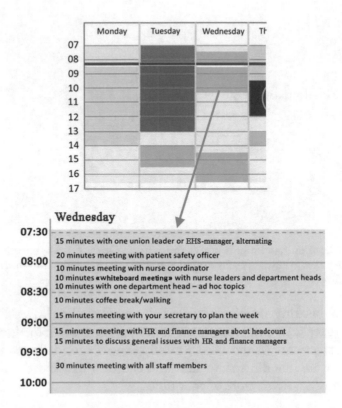

**Fig. 4.6** Efficient meeting schedule for a division head: In less than 3 hours you meet a large number of your subordinate leaders and administrative staff. Color coding is explained in Fig. 4.4. Copyright: Otto A. Smiseth

**Annual Strategy Meeting** Preferably at least 9 months prior to the subsequent budget year. For a division, all department and section heads, plus key members of the administrative staff should participate. Having one or two representatives for the patient organization to attend the meeting is positive. This is typically a full-day meeting or lunch-to-lunch meeting. Not the least, the social interaction during a lunch or dinner serves to build good relations between leaders.

**Budget Meetings** To plan next year's budget, it is useful to have 2–3 budget meetings where all the leaders in the division meet. The first meeting should be of more general character and the next one or two meetings should be more detailed. It is recommended to include not only department heads, but also section heads so that the people who shall do the job are involved in the planning. Typically, two hour's meetings.

## 4.4.3   Additional Meetings

**Meeting the Environmental Health and Safety Manager** The role of the Environmental Health and Safety (EHS) manager is to contribute to prevent injury and sickness to happen among the employees. They sometimes pick up problems which you should know about and which need a solution. I have been practicing regular meetings with the EHS manager, 15 minutes one-on-one meetings every second week and I find them useful.

**Meeting the Union Leaders** In some of the European countries the labor unions have a strong position. In these countries, it can be useful with regular dialogue meetings between the division head and the union leaders. I do this as a monthly, 1–2 hours meeting with all union leaders at division level. Both division head and HR manager attend. This is a combination of information and discussion meetings. It is also part of the listening strategy.

I also have a brief one-on-one meeting with the leader of one of the major unions every second week (Fig. 4.6).

**Meeting with the Patient Organizations** The division head and a small group of senior medical doctors and nurses meet the patient representatives. The meeting is chaired by the leader for the patient representatives. Frequency could be at least every second month.

## 4.5    Energize the Organization

**Daily Whiteboard Meetings** In my capacity as division head, I meet every morning for 10 minutes with all department heads and the leaders of the wards and intensive care units. I consider this my most important meeting. On the whiteboard or digital board, each nurse leader enters the number of available beds and number of nurses present at their unit (Fig. 4.7). The meeting is chaired by me as the division head. An important topic on the agenda is how to use the available capacity. If one units lacks nurses, the other units try to help. If there is risk that an operation may be cancelled due to lack of capacity at a postop unit, the other units try to help. These are great meetings which serve to optimize manpower use from day to day and are used to avoid surgery cancellations. Furthermore, at these meetings your subordinates get to know you and your expectations.

**Walking and Smiling** I recommend you take a walk through most units of your division each week. You may spend only 5 minutes at each place. You say hello, meet your people with a friendly smile and sometimes you

**Fig. 4.7** From "whiteboard meeting." These are daily 10 minutes capacity meetings every morning where the division head meets all the department heads and the nurse leaders. Copyright: Otto A. Smiseth.

would sit down and have a coffee. If you have 10–20 sections, it will take a couple of hours a week. You give the employees a feeling that you care for them and they will be more supportive to you as their leader. Even when there is a busy schedule, the walking around should be given high priority. I can guarantee it will be a success.

# Reference

Perlow, L. A., Noonan Hadley, C., & Eun, E. (2017). Stop the meeting madness. How to free up time for meaningful work. *Harvard Business Review. From the Magazine*, July–August 2017.

# 5

# Take Control of Finances

**Abstract** For many clinical leaders, the struggle to solve budget problems is frustrating and takes too much of their attention. To get control of finances, it is essential that clinical leaders understand the basics of hospital financing, and are up to date on key metrics, which include clinical activity data, numbers of employees and material costs. These insights should be used to take action whenever financial result is not according to budget plans. This chapter discusses and presents practical advice on how to take control over finances.

The chapter also discusses hospital financing in a society perspective and reviews OECD data, which show that current trends in hospital expenses are not sustainable. The chapter gives insights into what are the major inefficiencies in hospital services and suggests how society should meet the challenges.

Traditional as well as novel methods for hospital financing, such as value-based payment and bundled payment, are discussed. The chapter also discusses what should be expected from good clinical leaders when it comes to handling financial challenges and what their superior should expect. The chapter explains the importance of attitude for becoming a good leader, and how wrong attitude and disloyalty can make leaders unsuitable for their job.

What often makes the job as clinical leader cumbersome and frustrating is the feeling of being continuously chased by the hospital director and the hospital finance director. Throughout the budget year, there is a continuous struggle to respond with new measures to bring the financial result in balance and according to the budget. This dance seems to never end and takes too much of your time as leader. To get on the top of this chase, and free up time to be leader and not only an accountant, the solution is to take control over the finances in your own unit.

> After a couple of years as department head I was able to take control over finances, and from then on, I could execute my real job as leader, and not only work like a frustrated accountant.

To become a master of hospital finances does not require deep insights into economy. Some knowledge is required, however, and what you need is reviewed in this chapter. More important that economic theory is accurate and frequently updated metrics on clinical activity, on manpower use and on other expenses.

After I obtained more insights into metrics and finances, it was easier to understand what was going on, and I could much easier find solutions or respond logically to requests from the hospital director. The financial results could still be negative, but I had insights which gave me the confidence I needed to believe in my own solutions. Furthermore, I could more easily understand and support my subordinate leaders to find solutions when they had financial deficits. The following paragraphs describe how to get this control.

## 5.1   Macro Perspective: Big Challenges

Currently the USA spends about 18% of its annual gross domestic product (GDP) on health. In 2015, this amounted to $3.2 trillion, a figure equal to Germany's economy. Health spending growth has outpaced growth of the US economy. Most other peer countries spend about 10% of their GDP on health, which is much less than what the US spends. Still, the American health is, by most metrics, no better than that of other rich countries.

Health consumption expenditures
as a percent of GDP, 1970-2019

Relative contributions to total
national health expenditures, 2019

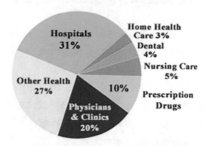

**Fig. 5.1** Left, total national health expenditures as a percent of Gross Domestic Product, 1970–2019. Right, relative contributions in the USA from hospitals and other services. Source: KFF analysis of OECD and National Health Expenditure (NHE) data. Get the data PNG. Does not include investments in structure, equipment, or research. Peterson KFF Health System Tracker

Why is it that health care in the US is much more expensive, but apparently no better than in other Western countries?

According to National Center for Health Statistics, the largest health expense is hospital care. As shown in Fig. 5.1 (right panel), hospital and physician services represent half of total health spending. Labor is the largest single cost component and makes up roughly 50 percent of total operating costs for most US hospitals (Deloitte, 2017). In some European countries, labor cost makes up an even larger fraction of operating cost, up to 60–70% of total costs.

A few decades ago, American health care spending was much closer to that of peer nations, so why is total health cost in the USA now so different from other countries?

"It's The Prices, Stupid"

This answer is from an article by Anderson et al. (2003). The study was repeated in 2019 and the answer was the same; that higher cost of health care in the USA than in other OECD countries was due to higher prices. People in the USA typically use about the same amount of health care as people in other wealthy countries, but pay a lot more for it (Anderson et al., 2019). All available data are consistent with these conclusions.

US health care is more expensive due to higher administrative cost and more use of expensive technologies.

Higher prices of health care in the USA compared to other OECD countries is in part explained by administrative costs which are related to the complexity of the country's health care system. The other important factor is that doctors in the USA apply more advanced technologies, including more use of novel imaging tools such as PET, CT, and MRI. They also use more expensive pharmaceuticals. It is not evident that using the most novel and often most expensive technologies always results in better health outcomes. In fact, health status is not better in the USA than in other Western OECD countries.

Whereas high health expenses is a challenge, there is also a positive effect on industry. The overall value added by the US biopharmaceutical industry, and its contribution to US GDP, is substantial, with a total value-added impact exceeding $625 billion, accounting for 3.2 percent of US GDP (TEConomy Partners, LLC, 2019). Furthermore, the bio-medical industry directly and indirectly supported more than 4.0 million US jobs in 2017.

The high price level of US health care is a driver for important health innovations such as new pharmaceuticals and therapies which lead to better life quality and reduction in mortality from diseases. Furthermore, it is argued that countries which criticize the US health care system, should be aware that high prices are not all bad for consumers, including themselves. The innovations and investments in new health technology which are stimulated by potential for future profit, confers benefits to patients globally. The *USA* is the *global leader* in science and technology, and medical innovation not only creates life-saving drugs, but also boosts the US economy. Though it is reasonable to push back on high health care prices, there may be a limit to how far this should be enforced.

High prices is an immediate challenge for customers, but stimulates invest-ments in health technologies which lead to better medicine long term.

In most countries, access to health care is considered a human right, and it is a challenge when health care is not affordable to everybody. The high prices of health services in the USA aggravates the problem that a significant fraction of the population has limited access to health care. Control and combat of the high health care prices may require changes in the system as well as focus on productivity and efficient utilization of new technologies. It is beyond the scope of this book to discuss health politics.

**Manpower as Cost Driver** Whereas in the USA the main reason for large and rising health budgets is prices, in several other OECD countries, it is apparent that control of manpower is the major challenge. As illustrated in Figs. 5.2, 5.3, and 5.4, the number of health workers has increased markedly over the last several years and is expected to increase further in the years to come, in part due to the aging population. *Between different wealthy countries, there is large unexplained variability in manpower use. This may indicate potential for improving effectiveness*

Figures 5.2, 5.3, and 5.4 are from the 2019 edition of the OECD publication Health at a Glance, and show large variability in manpower use between OECD countries. As expected, some of the low- or moderate-income countries have lower employment in the health sector than wealthier countries. What is difficult to explain, however, is why a number of wealthy European countries which, according to OECD statistics, have relatively similar health status, show large differences in manpower use. For example, Switzerland and some of the Nordic countries have 40–70% more nurses per capita than Canada, France, and the Netherlands. There are no suggestions in the OECD statistics that health status is any better in the former group of countries in spite of having the highest number of nurses per capita. As illustrated in Fig. 5.2, somewhat similar trends exist for total employment in social work and health service.

It is important to gain more insight into why different OECD countries with apparently similar health status, utilize manpower so differently. There is need for research into the contribution from mechanisms

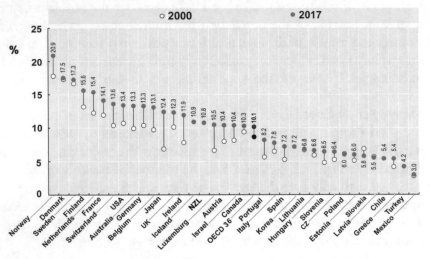

**Employment in health and social work as share of total employment, OECD countries 2000 and 2017 (or nearest year)**

**Fig. 5.2** Variations in social service and health workforce between OECD countries. Source: OECD Health Statistics 2019

such as different support systems, IT solutions and to what extent nurse assistants may be used differently.

One possibility is that social benefits such as sick-leave compensation may explain some of the differences. There is not extensive research on the topic, but one study identified large differences in annual days of sick-leave between some of the OECD countries (Hemmings & Prinz, 2020). When relating findings in the latter study to the OECD data shown in Fig. 5.3, however, there was no suggestion that number of sick days was an important contributor to the variability in manpower use between the countries. The issue should be looked into in more detail before a conclusion can be made regarding the impact of social benefits on manpower use in the health service.

Unfortunately, issues about professional efficiency are sensitive, and politician may be concerned with touching the topic in fear of losing support from the large group of voters employed in healthcare. On the other hand, one should avoid the premature conclusion that all the differences

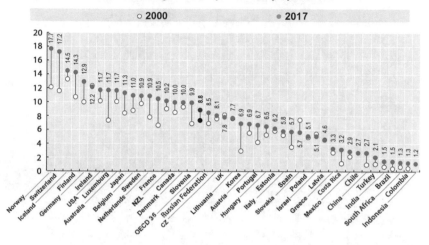

**Practising nurses per 1 000 population**

○ 2000          ● 2017

**Fig. 5.3** Data include not only nurses providing direct care to patients, but also those working in the health sector as managers, educators, researchers, etc. Austria and Greece report only nurses employed in hospital. Comparison of years 2000 and 2017. Source: OECD Health Statistics 2019

in manpower use reflect "true" inefficiencies. Hopefully, governments will provide resources to explore this by unbiased research. Obviously, just employing more health workers is not a sustainable solution.

**Technology as Cost Driver** When industry introduces new medical technologies and pharmaceuticals with potential to improve people's quality of life, it should of course be applauded. In many cases, however, the novel methods are more costly than traditional alternatives, and may therefore be challenging for hospital budgets.

A quality control system for implementation of new medical innovations is international clinical practice guidelines. These are developed by the leading medical experts and organizations in each medical specialty. For medical doctors, the guidelines represent the most important basis for deciding which drug, device, or surgery to use in clinical practice. These guidelines are produced jointly or separately by medical organizations in the USA, Europe, and Japan. Other countries and regions may

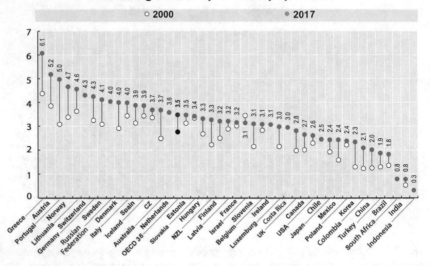

**Fig. 5.4** Data refer to all doctors licensed to practice. Data include not only doctors providing direct care to patients, but also those working in the health sector as managers, educators, researchers, etc. (adding another 5–10% of doctors). Comparison of years 2000 and 2017. Source: OECD Health Statistics 2019.

make their own guidelines or adapt previously published guidelines for use in their own countries.

> Most clinical practice guidelines are based only on medical effectiveness and do not consider cost-effectiveness

Most clinical practice guidelines, however, are limited to considering medical effectiveness without taking into account cost. The logic behind this is that different countries have different economic strength, and which drugs to use depends on the financial situation in each country. Furthermore, the medical doctors who write the guidelines, are experts only on medicine, and their mandate is exclusively to summarize the medical evidence. As a leader in a hospital, it is important to consider both cost and medical effectiveness. Then the decision about which medicines to use is often different than when considering medical effectiveness only. In different OECD countries, the economic strength differs, as reflected in different use of novel expensive medicines and technologies.

**Ambulatory Surgical Centers: A Cost-Reducing Trend** In the USA and some other Western countries, there is a large migration of patients from traditional hospitals to *ambulatory surgical centers,* which are facilities located either within a hospital setting or as independent units outside hospitals. At these centers, the patients get same-day surgery, which means entering and leaving the same day, with recovery in their home. The word ambulatory means walking, reflecting that patients are able to walk and are not confined to bed. The use of ambulatory surgical centers is stimulated by new developments within minimally invasive surgery.

The ambulatory surgical centers perform similar surgeries and interventions as in outpatient units inside hospitals. At the ambulatory surgical centers, however, procedures are done at substantially lower cost. From both a patient and a provider point of view, this trend is favorable. Outpatient and ambulatory healthcare services are predicted to be one of the fastest growing US industries towards 2030.

Some surgeries are complex, requiring multiple specialists in the teams, and sometimes there is need for recovery in intensive care units, and therefore these surgeries cannot be done at ambulatory surgical centers. The majority of surgeries and interventions, however, are less demanding and are well suited for ambulatory surgical centers. This includes orthopedic, plastic, peripheral vascular, urologic, ophthalmic, and oral surgery.

> An important cost reducing trend is migration of patients from traditional hospitals to ambulatory surgical centers.

Patient safety is an issue for isolated centers and in the USA, to comply with federal and state regulations, the ambulatory surgical centers need patient transfer agreements with local hospitals in case of severe complications and other emergencies.

**Taken together,** the OECD statistics show that rising national health expenses is a major challenge for most countries. This trend is not sustainable, and calls for new solutions.

In the years to come, there will be more use of personalized medicine with specific drugs targeted to each individual and their genotype. This type of tailored therapy is more costly than a traditional strategy based on a "one size fits all" concept, and will cause further rise in health care expenses. Of course, patients expect to receive state-of-the-art therapy, and it will be an ethical challenge if they are denied access to life-saving medicine while hospital inefficiencies persist.

There are good reasons, as indicated by the OECD data discussed in this chapter, that manpower use should be a main target for improved efficiency. There is also good reason to consider changes in the way hospitals are managed and organized internally and in the society. This includes consideration of shifting more patients from traditional hospital care to more efficient ambulatory surgical centers. Appropriate and efficient use of novel technologies is also important. As discussed in other chapters in this book, there are many possible solutions to improvement of hospital management, which can free up resources for providing funding for novel, efficient therapies.

## 5.2   Core Curriculum of Hospital Finance

All clinical leaders should understand the basics of hospital finance. When you read the subsequent paragraphs, you will understand that finance requires continuous attention from you as leader. It is all very simple, and you do not need dedicated training in economics to be a master of hospital finance.

The following chapters will first briefly review the essential theory of hospital financing, and then it is explained how to obtain budget control.

## 5.3   Capitation and Fee for Service

In principle, there are two different systems for hospital financing, *capitation*, and *fee for service*. Capitation means there is a fixed payment made periodically to the hospital from the provider. In general, when a hospital is financed by capitation, increased demand for health services within a budget year does not lead to more funding. You have to wait until the next budget year and hopefully get more funding then. If you, on the other hand, have fewer patients than planned, the financial

> Hospital financing by capitation gives control of cost, but due to lack of incentives, productivity tends to suffer.

result may be positive, which is an adverse incentive, as low activity is rewarded. Therefore, capitation may encourage providers to deliver less health care than needed. This is bad for productivity and may lead to long waiting times.

Fee for service means you are reimbursed for each patient you treat. With this system of financing, increasing clinical activity means more revenue. The challenge is that expenses also go up, and unless you have control of expenses, the result can be financial deficit. One should also be aware that high degree of fee for service financing makes the hospital and its units vulnerable when there are sudden and long-lasting reductions in patient referrals.

> Hospital financing by fee for service is good for productivity provided rigorous cost control.

With the fee for service model, there will be more incentive to speed up activity. Some health care providers, however, put a cap on the maximum number of DRGs (see next section) that will be reimbursed, and therefore total expense may be controlled in both models. In the USA, different modifications of the fee for service models are currently implemented and a strong trend is increasing use of value-based care, as discussed in more detail in Sect. 5.5.

A challenge with the fee for service model is that it may be misused if there is too much focus on quantity and not enough attention to quality of care. Furthermore, it can be a stimulus to add tests and treatments that are not strictly necessary. Therefore, fee for service financing may lead to overtreatment.

A study from the USA, where fee for service systems are widely used, indicated that fear of malpractice was the most common reason for over-treatment (Lyu et al., 2017). In that study, which was based on the opinions of medical doctors, another reason for over-utilizing tests and procedures was pressure from patients. Furthermore, difficulties with access to prior medical records was a reason for adding tests that were already done.

A challenge with fee for service is that physicians may be tempted to do unnecessary procedures when they personally profit from it. This is something which both the local clinical leaders and the health care providers should keep an eye on. On the other hand, flat salary systems with lack of incentives may lead to under-utilization of evidence-based medicine.

Professional medical societies publish *appropriate care documents* which give recommendations regarding diagnostic procedures and therapies for specific diseases. These documents complement the clinical practice guidelines, which essentially summarize scientific evidence. Every clinical leader should be up to date on these documents, and should take action when there is overuse or underuse of diagnostic tests or therapies. In addition, the provider may want to create stimuli to shift financing towards procedures which are evidence-based and reduce financing of those which have weaker documentation of utility. In some countries, such shift of funding is part of the annual adjustment of DRG-weights. This is an advantage of the fee for service model, which is not easily achieved when hospitals are financed by capitation.

As explained later in this book, when clinical leaders are dedicated to their job, are updated on what is appropriate standards of care, and systems for metrics are up and running, fee for service is an excellent model for securing both high productivity and control of finances. In hospitals or departments with limited steering information and poor management, however, fee for service is challenging and can easily lead to financial problems with negative effects on clinical services. In such hospitals, capitation may be better. In some hospitals, there may be a combination model with a component of fixed payment and fee for service on top.

Specialties like oncology, orthopedics, gynecology, and several others are well suited for fee for service. General internal medicine and pediatrics may need at least a substantial financing component of fixed payment or capitation. Importantly, there must be systems in place to ensure that patients with chronic illnesses, those who need extended care, and conditions with low reimbursement (DRG), are taken well care of.

Stick to your hospital's core values, and do not allow the fee for service system to restrict guideline-recommended therapies to patients with low reimbursement.

When it comes to psychiatry, where the resources needed for each patient are often unpredictable, it is obvious that fee for service has significant limitations.

## 5.4   Hospital Payment Based on Diagnosis

In some countries fee for service is based on a pricing system where each diagnosis or groups of diagnosis, (diagnosis-related groups, DRG) has a fixed price. The price for the different diagnosis is set according to the expected average cost of the hospital stay. Each diagnosis or groups of diagnosis is given a DRG weight or number, which reflects the estimated cost per patient with a specific diagnosis. The hospitals are reimbursed a fixed price per DRG produced.

The idea behind the "DRGs" is to identify the "products" that a hospital provides. In principle, 1 DRG is the cost of treating the average patient, but because different diagnosis demand different resources, there are many different DRGs. Heart transplantation may give 50 points and PCI (opening coronary artery by balloon or stent) could be 2 DRG points, reflecting that heart transplantation is about 25 times more costly than a PCI.

Productivity can be measured as the cost of producing one DRG.

The DRG-system was developed to replace a previously used reimbursement system which was "cost based." DRGs are assigned by a "grouper" program based on ICD (International Classification of Diseases) diagnoses, procedures, age, sex, discharge status, and the presence of complications or comorbidities. DRGs have been used in the USA since 1982 to determine how much Medicare should pay the hospital for each "product," assuming that patients with the same diagnosis on average consume similar hospital resources.

The use of DRG in hospital financing has significant limitations. First, DRG is meant for total hospital financing and is not sufficiently accurate to give correct pricing in the smaller units inside the hospital. Therefore, financing of departments and sections should not be based only on the DRG points they generate themselves.

Second, DRG points for specific diagnosis may change suddenly, and then your financial plan may collapse. One year I experienced with only a few months warning, a 50% reduction of the DRG for a diagnosis which represented one of my largest patient volumes. This meant 50% reduction in revenue. Since total DRG in the hospital remained the same, some of the other divisions got an unexpected increase in DRG. For my part, this was managed by getting funds transferred from the hospital director and we were able to continue.

Therefore, always work towards becoming more efficient, but focusing only on the DRG as revenue is risky. A limitation of the DRG-system is that it does not take into account quality of the services. That will be discussed in the following section.

## 5.5    Hospital Payment Based on Value

A system named *value-based payment* is designed to take into account both quality and cost of care. Value may be defined as improvement in health outcome from the patient perspective, and cost should include total cost to the purchaser, both short- and long-term. In some countries, elements of value-based payment are implemented to some extent.

A big challenge for value-based payment is how to measure the *value*, which means health outcome and not just indices of the care processes. Value-based payment can be part of fee for service and can also be incorporated as one of the factors that determine the budget in capitation financing.

*Bundled payments* represent a model with elements of value-based care with incentives for good coordination of care both inside and outside hospitals, better outcomes and lower costs. The meaning of the term bundled is that several services are bundled together, and there is a fixed price for the entire "*bundle*." Thus, with bundled payments, there is a predetermined target price for each episode of care. The target price includes not only costs of the initial hospital stay, but also costs of complications and hospital readmissions. In one version of this model, the provider takes on the risk to cover costs which exceed the target price for an episode of care. In case the episode turns out to be cheaper than the target price, the provider gets a share in the savings, provided quality is as expected.

One reason why bundled payments may be good, is to prevent premature discharge of patients who need more comprehensive care at the hospital. If they are discharged too early, it puts more load on the local health service and the patient may be readmitted for the same condition. In some systems, hospitals are paid for every single visit and therefore may be tempted to exploit it by early discharge, and benefit financially from the readmissions. With bundled payment, all health care related to one disease episode is covered by a standard price.

To what extent bundled payments contributes to efficient care is not really settled and is debated (Agarwal et al., 2020). Although the intensions behind bundled payments are good and may work well for a limited number of diseases, it remains to be shown that this model achieves the wanted results in wider groups of patients.

## 5.6    You Need to Read This Brief Theory

Every leader needs to understand a few simple terms and concepts such as fiscal year, budget, variance, and forecast. A *fiscal year* is any 12-month period that may not end on December 31. A fiscal year may end on March 31, for instance. Then the fiscal year would start on April 1. In hospitals, the fiscal year often is the same as the calendar year, starting on January 1. In this book, the term "*budget year*" is used regardless of starting date.

A *budget* is a financial plan for 12 months or another period. In a hospital, there is typically a master budget for the entire hospital and budgets for each division and department and for each section within the departments.

Each month the finance team presents financial results where the two most important components in the report are *variance* and *forecast*. Variance is the difference between planned result in the budget and actual result. The phrase "budget vs. actual" may be used when comparing the two.

In a monthly report, there is also a *forecast,* which is the predicted result at the end of the budget year. The forecast is based upon results at the time of the report and incorporates effects of plans for the remaining months of the year. The forecast is a very important parameter since it tells you how big financial challenge you have. If there is a negative forecast, you as leader are expected to take action and come up with measures to correct the predicted deficit.

> During monthly financial reports, the main focus should be on the forecast since it can and should be used to take immediate action.

Budgets are divided into the *operational budget* and *capital budget.* The operational budget is what "bothers" the leader continuously and is the detailed plan for annual revenues and expenses.

The capital budget is about investment in equipment, infrastructure such as IT and buildings. Construction of the capital budget has its own process, which typically involves the hospital owner.

In some hospitals, the leaders are asked to propose *business cases* which means smart investments that are good for patients and also give acceptable financial return. The term *business* means that there is expected a net positive financial result of the investment. The business cases are based upon cost and revenue over a few years, not just one budget year.

## 5.7  Know Your Metrics

Every month, leaders of divisions, departments, and sections receive a financial report showing results for the last month and cumulated results for the preceding months. If you are in balance, you can relax about economy, but often the budget vs. actual shows a deficit. In the latter case, you summon a meeting with your finance manager who will help you understand why you have a deficit. When you subsequently meet with your superior, the expectation from him is that you not only can explain the deficit, you should also present a plan for how to bring your economy in balance. In general, the reasons for a negative financial result are either too low activity (fee for service), use of too expensive materials or too many people employed.

When you meet with your superior, it looks really bad if you do not understand why you have a negative financial result, as it may indicate you have no control of the situation. It looks much better if you can explain why you have the negative result, and of course even better if you also present a plan for how to bring the result back in balance. It is very frustrating for your superior when he sees that you do not know the essentials about your unit.

> When meeting with your superior at a follow-up meeting, it looks really bad if you do not understand why you have a negative financial result. Knowing your metrics makes you much stronger.

## 5.8    The Good, the Bad, and the Ugly

The way most hospitals function is that the department head meets with the section heads each month, and together they review the activity and financial result. Prior to these meetings, you as department head should have a quick look at the activity card and the expenses for each one of the sections you will be reviewing. You meet with the section heads to get their view on the situation, and you should expect that they propose and take action according to the financial forecast. To make this into efficient meetings, they should be with one leader at a time. You may also have a meeting with all leaders, but this rarely gives you what you need since the group tends to act defensively, and good initiatives may be lost in the group thinking. When there is a financial deficit, they easily start complaining about the situation rather than coming up with actions points for themselves.

> In monthly reviews of financial result, you should meet only one leader at a time. If you meet several leaders, it often sets up some awkward group psychology where everybody feels sorry for everybody.

The following three cases illustrate how leaders respond differently to financial challenges:

**Case 1: The Good** At the monthly follow-up meeting called by the department head, the section head of a surgical unit meets to present the results from the last month, including financial results. Clinical results are fine, but the section has a substantial negative financial result, larger than for the other sections in the department. The department head asks the section head to explain why there is a deficit and what he will do to correct it. The section head knows his metrics well, and explains that the negative result is due to fewer surgeries than planned and therefore less revenue than in the budget. This is because two nurses were out of work that month, one due to chronic illness and one with unexpected health problems related to pregnancy. The nurses were experts in the operating room, and replacements had not been available. The section head then explained that in the remaining months of the budget year, he will increase surgical activity by changing the work hours for some of the other nurses, and they as well as the union representative had accepted this. The department head was of course very happy with the solution.

**Case 2: The Bad** In this case, at the monthly follow-up meeting of a diagnostic laboratory, there is a moderate negative financial result. The section head is not quite sure what went wrong, but expenses to diagnostic material were over the budget and there was less revenue than in the budget. She does not have data on numbers of diagnostic procedures. She does not know why the doctors used more expensive material than planned, but argues that medicine is complicated and she probably made the budget too slim, and therefore the budget is wrong. She is not sure why revenues were too low since every physician and every nurse had been busy the last month. When the department head asks what she will do to correct the problem, she responds that she will try to regulate expenses. She explains that all employees at the section were busy, and therefore it was difficult to see what could be done to increase activity.

**Case 3: The Ugly** The leader of a surgical unit meets with the department head, and is asked why there is such a large negative financial result. He does not know himself and points to the finance manager who is also present, to get help to explain the figures. She explains that the financial deficit is due to higher material expenses for different types of equipment and need for more nurses than in the budget. This section leader expresses that he was not aware of the high material expenses since he had not seen the figures prior to the meeting. He believes it may be due to some expensive surgical grafts which were recently introduced. He acknowledges that ideally these grafts should have been in the budget, but a recent clinical study had shown that these grafts were superior to the old ones. When he is asked if he can reduce expenses for the remaining months to correct the financial deficit, he argues that this is possible if the hospital director or politicians can tell him which patients shall get the old type of graft. He wants his patients to have the very best, and he will have a hard time convincing his doctors to lower quality by using the old type of graft. He is not sure who decided that more nurses were needed, and argues that he is not a nurse and does not have competence or authority to modify the way nurses work. Furthermore, he argues that it is the finance manager and not himself who is the expert on these financial issues.

When judging the quality and performance of these three section leaders, it is obvious that the leader in the first case took responsibility for his result, although the deficit was larger than for the other two, and he had a plan to bring the result in balance. Importantly, he knew his metrics and was well prepared for the meeting.

In the second case, there is a problem with the leader's attitude as she does not accept the budget and argues it is too small. This is bad for the morale in her section, in particular since she is the one who proposed and accepted the budget. With regard to solutions, she does not seem motivated to do what is needed. This leader also had a major weakness in not knowing her metrics. Since she was confused with regard to what caused the deficit, it was difficult for her to see a solution. This leader needs a one-on-one talk with her superior and should be coached about good leadership. The expectation should be to change attitude and take responsibility. She should be asked to come up with a plan to bring the finances in balance. A new follow-up meeting should be scheduled within a few days. If she then has not made a satisfactory plan, she should be offered help from someone else. If she does not want help, she should do something else and you find a new leader.

The third case is an obvious complete failure as leader. He happens to be one of the best surgeons in the hospital, but does not understand his role as leader. He is not willing to instruct the doctors to use the type of surgical graft he promised when he made the budget, and he is not willing to support the nurses and find solutions for how to improve their efficiency. Furthermore, he wants the hospital director to do the job he is paid to do himself, to find the optimal therapy for each patient. He clearly abdicates as responsible for finances and tries to move responsibility over to the finance manager. Fortunately, such poor leader performance is not frequent, but leaders often have elements of his bad attitudes. This leader should not get a second chance, as his attitudes are destructive for the morale in his section. Furthermore, since he is a well-known surgeon, he may also have bad influence on other leaders in the hospital.

## 5.9   Be Up to Date on Clinical Activity

The metrics you need to take control over finance are (1) clinical activity, (2) cost per procedure, and (3) number of employees. Let's start with metrics on clinical activity and address procedure cost and employee number in the next two sections.

The way I work, the administrative staff gives me a weekly report which covers all the major procedures and how we are doing compared to budget plans. Figure 5.5 shows an example of such a report.

When I receive this report, I can in less than five minutes, see how the entire division is doing. I have more than 20 different "production lines" in the weekly report. Fig. 5.5. shows an example of how activity metrics is presented. Manual entering of data takes a few minutes each week at the sections. By doing it themselves, the sections get ownership to the data. Since the people who take care of the patients have entered the data, I know they are correct.

| Activity data 2019 | Number of procedures performed | | | | | | | | | Deviation from budget | |
| | January | January | January | January | February | February | February | February | | | |
| Number of procedures | Week 1 | Week 2 | Week 3 | Week 4 | Week 5 | Week 6 | Week 7 | Week 8 | Sum | Procedures | DRG points |
| Open heart surgery | 14 | 17 | 20 | 20 | 20 | 20 | 16 | 20 | 147 | 5 | 30 |
| Lung surgery | 8 | 9 | 5 | 6 | 5 | 7 | 3 | 4 | 47 | -6 | -21 |
| PCI acute | 27 | 28 | 25 | 23 | 30 | 25 | 29 | 26 | 232 | 12 | 24 |
| PCI elective | 10 | 12 | 11 | 13 | 10 | 8 | 7 | 13 | 84 | -16 | -22 |
| Left heart catherization | 75 | 76 | 79 | 70 | 81 | 74 | 55 | 76 | 633 | 23 | 12 |
| Ablation atrial fibrillation | 21 | 22 | 23 | 21 | 23 | 22 | 14 | 22 | 168 | -17 | -85 |
| Pacemakers | 6 | 7 | 8 | 6 | 7 | 6 | 4 | 8 | 52 | 2 | 3 |
| ICD-pacemakers | 3 | 3 | 5 | 4 | 4 | 5 | 3 | 5 | 32 | -2 | -24 |
| Total | | | | | | | | | | | -83 |

**Fig. 5.5** Example of activity report card for a cardiovascular unit. The report card shows activity for each week. The cumulated activity after 8 weeks is shown in the column named "Sum." The next column to the right shows differences between actual and planned number of procedures after 8 weeks. The last column to the right shows deviation between planned DRG points in the budget and the actual number of points after 8 weeks. The DRG points reflect the revenue. Copyright Otto A. Smiseth

## 5.10    Be Up to Date on Procedure Cost

It is essential that you know the cost of the major medical procedures. This is important both for budget planning and for control of expenses during the budget year.

Figure 5.6 illustrates the relatively common challenge that cost suddenly increases because the doctors have started with a new medical product which is supposed to be superior to the traditional one. If you did not have cost per procedure, it would have been difficult to find out why expenses went up. The overuse of costly stents gave a financial deficit, which the leader had to solve the following months. For a hospital with fee for service financing, that could be done by increasing activity to get more revenue.

Most sections have many different procedures and unless you isolate each one of the big ones, it is hard to understand what is going on and how to react.

To build a system with regular updates on cost per procedure is a bit of work, and it is important that the finance manager gets freedom to dispose time to do this. Importantly, the section leaders must be involved

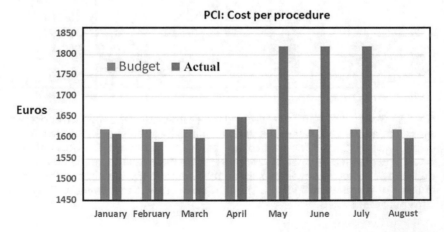

**Fig. 5.6** Monthly report on procedure cost for materials to do one PCI. Please note that from May actual cost exceeded cost in the budget. This was due to use of a new expensive stent which was not in the budget. In August the situation is under control. Copyright: Otto A. Smiseth

and use their doctors and nurses to identify all the material needed to do the procedures which goes into the spreadsheet used to calculate the cost. You do this only for procedures you know tend to get out of control.

When the spreadsheet with cost details for each procedure is made, it is very quick to update it when there are changes in prices for one or more products.

## 5.11   Be Up to Date on Employee Numbers

Since payroll is the largest expense for the hospital, it is essential that you are up to date on number of employees. This number is represented not only by employees in permanent positions, but also includes the employee equivalents represented by overtime, substitutes and all other expenses related to working hours. The number of employees in the latter category is calculated as the monthly expense to these extra personnel divided by the average salary for each category of employee. Of course total payroll gives essential information, but separating into permanent staff and employee equivalents gives you important additional insight.

> Payroll is the largest expense in hospitals, and therefore a strict system is needed for approving new employees.

In an ideal world, leaders at all levels in the hospital should have authority to employ nurses and doctors without asking their superior for approval. Unfortunately, this does not work, and therefore you need a system at a higher level to make these decisions.

I recommend having a *position committee* led by the division head, which makes all final decisions regarding new employees. The decisions are taken based on two kinds of metrics, financial result and number of employees the last month. By having the meetings weekly, the units get quick answers with little bureaucracy. Figure 5.7 illustrates how decisions are made. The finance manager has prepared and presents graphically the relevant data.

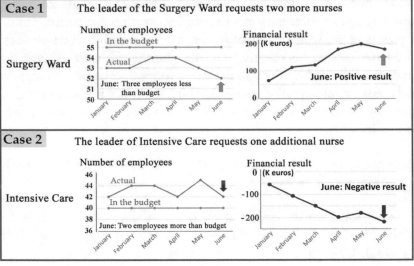

**Fig. 5.7** Position committee meeting: In Case 1, use of manpower and financial result are within budget, and the request for two more nurses is accepted. In Case 2, the result is not according to budget, and the request for one additional nurse is rejected. Financial results shown in the figure represents the cumulated result from start of the budget year. Copyright: Otto A. Smiseth

Case 1 is an application from a section which wants 2 extra nurses. This section has a positive financial result and uses fewer employees than in the budget. This section gets the application approved without need for further discussion.

Case 2 is from a section which wants an extra nurse. For this section, the finance report shows a negative result, and they use two nurses more than in the budget. Therefore, this application is rejected based on the objective data presented.

To make the process fair, the applicant is allowed to appeal the decision, and if she does, there is need for an additional meeting to discuss the matter in more detail. At this appeal meeting, the department head who is responsible for the section should meet personally. She should explain with appropriate metrics, why extra staff is needed, and what can be done to improve efficiency in the unit. Potentially, they do not need the extra nurse if the unit becomes more efficient. The key message here is that the leader should always think improvement in productivity before considering hiring new employees.

There are, however, cases such as unexpected increase in patient referrals in the middle of the budget year, when it may be necessary for medical reasons to employ additional people. Be aware, however, that you do not convert temporary needs for more manpower into more permanent positions. If you do not keep an eye on this, it will be a driver for rise in number of employees and fall in efficiency. It is much harder to reduce the number of employees than to say yes when your subordinates ask for an increase.

When an application for a new employee is accepted, who will get the job should be decided at a lower level where the leader knows best which qualifications are needed. Importantly, when the job is a leader position, the decision should always be made in agreement with the leader one level up. These positions are always very important, and hiring the wrong leader, can have long-lasting negative effects.

Furthermore, when employing new people, salaries higher than standard, should also be decided by the division head, and not at section or department level. Because people tend to tell colleagues what their salary is, local inflation of salaries can spread to other places in the organization. Therefore, when a local leader is "kind" to one employee, others will soon know and will demand the same salary. The HR manager should have a controller function on salary standards.

## 5.12    Flat Budget Cuts Are Demoralizing

When hospitals have financial problems, the hospital director should avoid enforcing flat budget cuts in the clinical units. It is a sign of poor management when units with high productivity get the same cuts as those with lower productivity and larger potential for improvement. This is demoralizing, in particular when the units which are most productive know that some units just do not care.

Undifferentiated, flat cuts weaken motivation to improve efficiency since productive departments know that they anyway get similar cuts as the sloppy departments.

## 5.13    Keep Your Finger on the Pulse

The whiteboard meeting, which is discussed in Sect. 4.5, is a very efficient way of getting daily updates on clinical activity and meeting your leaders. For several years I have practiced this type of daily capacity meeting, and it gives a fantastic dialogue between the division head an all the clinical leaders. The meeting takes only 10 minutes and sorts out many of the daily operational challenges. If attendance is not good, do not accept it, presence should be obligatory for your subordinate leaders. To make this brief meeting at the busiest time of the day attractive, I also use the meeting to come with brief "hot news" from the hospital management. This increases motivation to attend the meeting since nobody like to miss key information.

## 5.14    The Role of the Finance Manager

The finance manager prepares the budget based on activity plans coming from the clinical leaders. During the budget year, she provides the data the clinical leaders need to make decisions. She also takes care of controller function of finances.

Importantly, the finance manager is not responsible for finances, she only provides support to the leaders. It is the leaders of clinical units who are responsible for the budget and the financial result.

The finance manager should not be a passive accountant, but should be proactive, and help the leaders with generation of metrics on clinical activity and other reports.

The finance manager and her team are among the most valuable people in the division. Since finances take up so much of the leader's time, it is essential to have the right people in these positions. To make the finance team efficient, they should be given independency and authority to make decisions within their areas of responsibility. It takes time to build the quality and efficiency you need in this small team, but with the right people in these positions, they will become your most important helpers.

## 5.15   Avoid Fragmentation of Responsibility

In a professional organization, the hospital director delegates full responsibility to subordinate leaders, as illustrated in Fig. 5.8a. This implies that the hospital director trusts the leaders as responsible for both finances and clinical services. To follow up that the job is done properly, the hospital director has monthly and quarterly report meetings with the division heads.

Unfortunately, it happens that the hospital director does not trust the division heads as responsible for finances, and therefore establishes an extra control line to "inspect" the daily operations done by the division heads. This is done by letting the finance manager in the division report to the hospital director via the finance director, instead of reporting to the division head. I am amazed to see how silently such a system which violates basic principles of line management may be introduced. It is in fact a signal from the hospital director that he does not trust his leaders.

Of course, the only appropriate way of reporting is that the finance manager reports to the division head, who in turn reports to the hospital director. With the extra control line, the finance manager becomes a

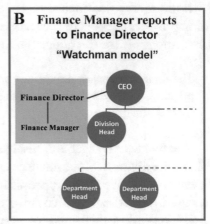

**Fig. 5.8** Panel (a): Organization where leaders have full responsibility. Panel (b): Organization where the finance manager bypasses the division head and reports to the hospital director via the finance director. In this case the finance manager acts as a "watchman" to control the division head. This is a sign of mistrust to the judgment of the division head. Copyright: Otto A. Smiseth

"watchman" who is there to check that the division head does nothing wrong. This model can strengthen the feeling which some clinical leaders have, that budget and finances is not their problem, but is something which the finance people have to deal with.

It is important that the finance manager works closely with the division head. In the small administrative team at the division, which also should include the HR manager, there has to be 100% trust and loyalty. The model shown in Fig. 5.8b will ruin the efficiency of this team.

> The best model is that the finance manager at division level reports to the division head rather than to the central finance director.

Since the finance teams are small at division and department level, and usually below "critical mass" for building new professional competence, it is important that everybody in the hospital working with finance are in regular contact. This is necessary to be up to date on systems and new developments within their field of expertise.

When it comes to customizing metrics and reports needed for your division, it is the finance manager and her team which produces these for you. You should be clear on your expectations, which must be that the finance manager gives top priority to production of the metrics you want. With the organizational model shown in Fig. 5.8b, this is difficult since the finance manager then will give priority to requests from the Finance Director.

I have been very fortunate to work with some fantastic finance people who were clever with accounting, but also became true experts in building and producing metrics. Importantly, as their leader, I had to invest time to build the team, and to give them frequent feedback.

## 5.16 Hunt Down the Big Five

Planning and coordination of resources are important for patient management and efficiency in hospitals. Some hospitals do this very well, while others have large potential for improvement. When you are stuck and find no solution to the budget deficit, and the employees complain that they cannot run any faster, look for the major inefficiencies. There are five areas for improvement which are most obvious, *the big five*.

1. **Inadequate preparations prior to admission**

Make sure preparations are done prior to hospitalization. In one of my most productive units, we found that a substantial fraction of the admissions ended with the patient becoming discharged due to inadequate preparation prior to the hospital stay. This included issues such as the patient did not want the therapy she was admitted for, the patient was not taking the medication she was supposed to take prior to the planned intervention, the patient had a flue, etc.

Have a competent nurse to call the patients prior to admission, to make sure everything is according to plans. I recommend the patient is contacted by telephone by a nurse who is familiar with the particular specialty, 2–3 weeks before admission, to ensure that everything is well planned. Another telephone call and a brief talk with the patient should be done the day before admission to check if everything is done as agreed and that no intercurrent illness has occurred. These two telephones take less than ten minutes per patient. In addition to better logistics, the patients feel much safer when they know that the hospital is well prepared for their arrival. Always have a list of patients who are prepared to come on a short notice when you have cancellations.

## 2. Intra-hospital waiting time

It happens too often that after admission, the doctors find out that they need tests which were not booked when the admission was planned. This could be simple tests like ultrasound or more advanced tests such as CT, CMR, and PET, which usually have limited capacity, and if not pre-booked, patients may spend time inside the hospital to get the test done. This additional internal waiting time can vary from a few hours to a few days for each patient.

To optimize planning of the admission, let senior specialists look through the case prior to hospitalization and book relevant tests. It helps to have a standardized program for all common diagnosis.

There are many highly competent nurses who know lots about the medical needs, who can do a great job with planning the stay of each patient. Have a couple of these nurses as coordinators. To attract the best nurses to these important positions, give them good deals, no night shifts and no weekends.

Another practical solution is to have a waiting zone next to the laboratories so that there is always a patient ready for the test when the previous patient is done. Then you save all the time which is wasted by calling the ward to bring the next patient. At the ward, the nurse must find the patient, who may not be in his room, and then she needs to call the transport service to bring the patient to the test laboratory.

Internal waiting can also be a problem for acute care and is more a safety concern. A frequent complaint is that acutely ill patients are brought to hospitals and their medical condition is deteriorating after arrival before they are finally seen by a doctor.

A large group which depends critically on hospital logistics is patients with heart attack (myocardial infarction), who need urgent treatment to prevent irreversible damage to their heart. After arrival at the hospital door, they need rapid transferal to the heart laboratory where a cardiologist can open their obstructed heart vessel with balloon and stent. The internationally accepted benchmark for this transferral is *door-to-balloon time*, which is the time from arrival at the hospital door until a balloon is inflated in the obstructed artery. As shown in a large study of patients admitted with acute myocardial infarction (STEMI), *door-to-balloon times* <45 minutes were associated with one-year mortality of 4.6%, and with *door-to-balloon times* between 90- and 360-minutes mortality increased to 17.5% (Park et al., 2019).

Many hospitals in USA and in other Western countries are struggling with logistics, and often have door-to-balloon times >90 minutes, whereas recommendations in clinical practice guidelines are <90 minutes. Hospitals with good logistics have average door-to-balloon times <30 minutes. Every hospital with >90 minutes average door-to-balloon time need to fix it since it is a threat to patent safety.

### 3. Online Booking

Everybody is accustomed to online booking for hotel rooms and appointment with the hairdresser. For the referring physician and patients, online booking for hospital services is also of great help. In terms of efficiency, however, the biggest saving with online booking is for intra-hospital use. By going online, you can see which time slots are available, and you select the best one for your patient. Importantly, when one test is booked, you can immediately move on, and book the next appointment for the patient.

With online booking, you do not need to make a phone call or send a mail to the referral unit and wait for confirmation. Furthermore, you can do booking 24/7, and you do not need to wait until the receptionist comes to work or is back from lunch.

In addition to saving lots of time for the secretaries or nurses, the referral unit can more easily fill up their capacity, which is great for their efficiency. Some hospitals already have systems for online booking.

If you still make booking inside the hospital with telephone and e-mail, switching to online booking will markedly improve efficiency.

The online appointment scheduling is often unpopular among the employees at the receiving unit of the booking because they lose control over their work day. Not only in this case, but always when the employees do an extraordinary effort which improves productivity, consider if something can be done which makes the work more enjoyable. What the employees often want, is time for education and improving their job skills.

## 4. Outpatient Care and Ambulatory Surgery

Outpatient care means patients are taken care of without staying overnight in a hospital, and is used for diagnostic evaluation, medical treatment, minor surgeries and minimally invasive surgery. Figure 4.2 shows an example of how outpatient care may be organized in a hospital. One should avoid mixing outpatient units and regular wards, however, since combination of the two models leads to loss of efficiency for the outpatient service. When compared to inpatient services, the cost saving with outpatient care is substantial. The cost is lower due to less need for nurses since there is no overnight stay, and there is typically more efficient logistics.

When doctors and nurses get used to combining hotel and outpatient care, they will soon discover that a large fraction of patients can be taken care of without being admitted to the hospital. This also includes patients who traditionally would be hospitalized for extended periods for diagnostic work-ups or initiation of medical therapy. To make the shift attractive to doctors and nurses, it is important to establish good room capacity and support service at the outpatient units. Squeezing doctors and nurses into outpatient units where they have to fight for rooms and with limited equipment is unlikely to be successful.

Obvious advantages for patients with staying in a hotel are more privacy, silence and rest than in a hospital. Modern patient hotels have space for a family member or other care partner to accompany the patient during the stay. This makes it possible for fragile patients who would otherwise need to be hospitalized, to stay in a patient hotel. It is also a good learning opportunity for the care partner who gets insights which can be useful when a patient needs help after discharge. For sick children, staying in a hotel or small apartment with family is much better for their mental health than staying alone in a hospital room.

The infrastructure needed for a modern patient hotel and up-to-date outpatient units have a significant cost, but as discussed in Sect. 5.26, the largest long-term cost of running hospitals is operative cost, and manpower represents the biggest fraction. Therefore, investments in hotel and outpatient infrastructure can give good financial returns due to less need for manpower compared to providing similar services inside hospitals. On top of that comes benefits for patients in terms of experienced quality.

As discussed in Sect. 5.1 ambulatory surgical centers which are organized as freestanding facilities located either within a hospital setting or outside, are even more efficient than outpatient units integrated into hospitals. In the USA, this is reflected in Medicare reimbursements which are much lower for services at ambulatory surgical centers than for similar procedures done at outpatient departments in hospitals. The prize difference for the same procedure can be around 50%, and in some cases even larger.

Patients prefer ambulatory surgical centers, as they allow "quick in and quick out," are more convenient, and there is lower risk of infections. Since most patients treated at ambulatory surgical centers have already undergone a diagnostic work up, they can be taken directly to the planned surgery or other procedure, and with this model for care, they leave the facility on the same day for recovery in their home. This model may also be combined with staying in hotel the night before and after the surgery. Similar to traditional hospitals, ambulatory surgical centers must have systems in place to ensure good patient safety and quality standards, and health outcome data must be available.

A shift from inpatient to outpatient care and ambulatory surgical centers represents one of the largest efficiency potentials for hospital medicine. Therefore, every hospital should consider to switch whenever it is feasible. Still, the transition is slow in many hospitals. To facilitate the switch, insurance companies and governments should establish financial incentives, which makes it attractive to make the transition. In fee for service systems, this should include proper DRG-weights for outpatient services and treatment at ambulatory surgical centers.

Shifting patients from inpatient to outpatient care combined with hotel, and using ambulatory surgical centers will markedly improve efficiency of hospitals.

Health providers may be concerned that ambulatory surgical centers, which typically have better availability than conventional hospitals, lead to inflation of treatment indications. In such cases and when governments want a cap on maximum number of procedures, a solution is that medical specialists working in hospitals determine treatment indications and refer patients to ambulatory surgical centers. A caveat with this solution is that government involvement tends to slow down processes and the result may be unacceptable waiting times. Hospitals may also consider partnership and in some cases ownership to ambulatory surgical centers.

Instead of clinging to the past, hospital leaders should adapt to the new reality and adjust their model to what is best for society and patients. Keeping artificially and unnecessarily high prices by having most of patient management inside conventional hospitals is definitely not sustainable.

There is much to learn from the classical article by Theodore Levitt on "Marketing Myopia" (1960). His philosophy was that businesses should define themselves based on the needs of the customer. To illustrate what he meant, he used US rail as one of several examples. This was one of the most successful industries in human history, and was thought to be an everlasting success. From the middle of the last century, however, US rail stopped growing and was gradually replaced by buses, taxes, automobiles, and airlines. The main lesson from this example is that customers did not care about the railway technology; all they wanted was safe, comfortable an affordable transport from their home, and all the way to the destination. Depending on convenience and cost, this could include combinations of trains, airplanes, buses, and taxis. US rail did not see the opportunity to expand their portfolio of services, but continued believing their business was railway (Levitt, 2004). Apparently, they could not see that their mission was passenger transport. This lack of vision in the business, not seeing the needs of the customers and where things were going, contributed to the fall of US rail.

This may be considered analogous to hospitals which stick to the traditional hospital model, and fail to adapt to the new reality that patients prefer ambulatory surgical centers as they are more comfortable and more affordable. For hospital planners, it is important to structure services according to the preferences of patients, and this implies considering a shift to more outpatient care and use of ambulatory surgical centers.

## 5. Surgery Cancellations

Cancellation of planned surgery is unfortunate for everybody, first of all for patient and family, but also represents a waste of resources and weakens hospital economy.

The magnitude of the problem and the causes differ between hospitals and between medical specialties. In general, cancellations rates are lower in hospitals doing only elective surgery as compared to those which also do emergency surgery. In some hospitals, structural factors such as insufficient capacity of postoperative and intensive care beds and limited operating room capacity explain many of the cancellations.

There are also several patient-related factors that contribute to surgery cancellations. This includes failure to comply with preoperative instructions, change in medical condition, loss of motivation for the operation and insufficient information prior to the surgery. Surgery cancellations for these reasons can be prevented by better preparation of patients prior to the surgery. As discussed above, this may include preoperative telephoning to check that the patient is well prepared, and additional checks one or two days before surgery at a patient hotel or an outpatient unit (Al Talalwah & McIltrot, 2019).

Mechanisms behind surgery cancellation became evident in Oslo when we merged three hospitals with markedly different cancellation rates for heart surgery. One hospital had essentially no cancellations as they did exclusively elective (non-acute) cardiac surgery. Therefore, surgery was never cancelled due to acute patients who had to be given higher priority. Furthermore, in this hospital, anaesthesiology was organized under the leadership of the head of heart surgery, and lack of anesthesia support was rarely an issue.

The second hospital in this merger, which did both elective and acute heart surgery, had just a few cancellations each month. One reason for low cancellation rates was that the anaesthesiologists served no other surgical departments than heart surgery. Therefore, there were hardly ever cancellations due to lack of anesthesia support. Furthermore, this hospital had a patient hotel staffed with a few nurses. Every elective patient would arrive in the hotel one or two days prior to the planned surgery and were carefully prepared and made ready for the operation. On the day of surgery, patients were brought directly from the hotel to the operating room.

The third hospital, which had a substantial fraction of acute heart surgery in-between the elective patients, had several surgery cancellations each month. Cancellation was often due to unexpected acute surgery or overfilled intensive care units with too low capacity. Furthermore, there was limited hotel capacity, and there was no dedicated outpatient unit where nurses could prepare patients for the surgery. Therefore, when patients arrived and were not ready, the surgery was cancelled, and patients would occupy hospital beds while additional tests or assessments were done. In other cases, they were discharged and were readmitted at a later time. Furthermore, in this hospital, the anaesthesiologists did not report to the head of heart surgery. Instead, they were employed at the Anaesthesiology Division, which served the entire hospital. With this model, the anesthesia service was outside the control of the leader of heart surgery.

So, what are the take-home messages from these three cases? Minimize surgery cancellations by doing the following: First, whenever feasible, make a shielded unit for high-volume elective surgery which is protected from interruption by acute surgery.

Second, make sure that all patients are well prepared and ready for surgery before arrival in the hospital. Third, rather than bringing patients directly into the hospital, use patient hotel in combination with outpatient units to do final checks and preparations. On the day of surgery, the patient is brought directly from the hotel to the operating room. If it turns out that a patient is not ready for surgery, another patient on a short notice list is contacted and brought in. This way, most elective patients spend a night in a patient hotel before they are admitted in the hospital.

Reduction of hospital stay by one night for most elective patients is a major saving and comes on top of the benefits of avoiding surgery cancellations. Some patients need more than one day in the hotel to be ready for surgery, and then the saving is even larger.

Fourth, for large surgical departments which depend heavily on intensive care, make the postoperative and intensive care units part of the surgical departments. Furthermore, for large surgical departments, it is most efficacious when the anesthesia is under the control of the leader of surgery.

For most hospitals, the operating rooms represent the dominant source of revenue. Therefore, it is essential for hospital finances that they are managed properly. This includes securing sufficient capacity for patients at the postoperative and surgical intensive care units. Restrictions on number of nurses at surgical intensive care units without considering lost revenue by fewer operations may hurt the economy.

Operating rooms represent the largest source of revenue in most hospitals, and it is therefore critical for global hospital economy that they are managed professionally.

The intensive care and operating room units are well suited to be responsibility centers, as discussed in Sect. 5.23. If leaders of these large economies are responsible for cost only (cost center model), without also being responsible for revenue (responsibility center model), it is a weakness of the system. When surgical intensive care units are organized as cost centers with no responsibility for revenue, large revenue may be lost. Of course, it is important to limit expenses, including salaries to nurses, but taking decisions regarding nursing staff without considering revenue makes no sense.

As I recommend in Sect. 5.23, all units in a hospital which generate revenue should be run as responsibility centers. Since operating rooms represent the dominant source of revenue in hospitals, it is essential that not only the medical service, but also finances are managed professionally in these units. How this can be done is explained in Sect. 5.23, using wards and intervention laboratory as example.

## 5.17   Doctors vs. Managers

Clinicians are trained to help patients and are dedicated to give individual patients the best possible care. To do this, they want autonomy and to apply the most recent evidence-based medicine. In particular when working in wealthy countries, doctors have a hard time accepting that resources should limit their capacity to improve life quality of sick people. Doctors more or less "get their orders" from the clinical practice guidelines and want to apply these when treating their patients. The managers, however, "get their orders" from the hospital director and finance director and do not allow more spending than in the budget.

Doctors and managers do and should think differently!

The fundamental challenge is to balance calls for a common set of values and the need to recognize that doctors and managers do and should think differently (Edwards & Marshall, 2003). If managers accept medical priorities without considering cost and budget, the health system would collapse. If doctors set budget balance as their primary objective when taking care of individual patients, regardless of medical consequences, the patients would suffer, and society would react.

The employees should understand that the duty of their leader is first, to ensure that the doctors and nurses get the budget they need to do their job, and second, to control that during the budget year, they spend no more money than at their disposal in the budget. If the doctors have forgotten to include a major expense in the budget, it is their own fault that the money is not available, it is not the fault of their leader or the finance manager. If new evidence comes up that an expensive medicine which is not in the budget, can save life, the doctors cannot start using it until decided by their leader, which could mean waiting until the next budget year.

Employees sometimes ask why finances are so important in a hospital since the mission of the hospital is to take care of sick people, not to make money. It is correct that most hospitals are either non-profit or owned by governments, and therefore making money is not a primary objective.

They need money, however, to buy new equipment, to have adequate staffing and to afford best available drugs. Therefore, with a negative financial result, the hospital may not afford to give their patients the best evidence-based medicine.

Sometimes employees argue that government is wasting money on unimportant things and therefore the hospital should get the financing they need. Apparently, they do not accept that changes in priorities between different areas in society are up to the politicians not the hospital director.

## 5.18   Be Professional with Evidence-Based Medicine

Hospital leaders have continuous pressure from the medical profession to apply new, promising medicines and technologies. A typical case is when doctors come back from a medical conference where new clinical studies were presented, which show there is a novel medicine that is superior to traditional therapy, and they want to start using it. To respond professionally to such pressure, there are a few things every clinical leader should know about evidence-based medicine and clinical studies.

In most countries, there are governmental committees which evaluate and approve new drugs and devices. In addition, medical specialties such as neurology, cardiology, oncology, and several others have international expert committees which produce clinical practice guidelines. These expert committees summarize current evidence and give recommendations regarding which therapies to use.

> Do not switch to a novel medicine unless it is supported by scientific evidence published in leading medical journals, and the technology has been put in context and is recommended by external expert committees.

As a general rule, never start with a new medicine or device unless there is strong evidence that it benefits patients. The evidence should be published in leading international medical journals since that means the study has been critically reviewed by experts in the field.

The highest level of clinical evidence is obtained in *randomized controlled trials*. In these trials, patients are selected by a random process, and bias is minimized by blinding the patients to which therapy they receive, active treatment or placebo. When feasible, the same applies to the doctors, who should not know whether their patients receive active treatment or placebo (double blind). The randomized controlled trials should preferably have clinical outcome as treatment goal. Ideally, the evidence should come from at least two different randomized controlled trials. This is because a single study may have weaknesses such as unrepresentative patient groups, selection bias, only short-term effects were studied, and in some cases, the observed effect may just be the play of chance which happens to be statistically significant.

In some cases, the evidence is considered sufficient with just one *randomized controlled trial,* provided it is supported by other studies, such as registry data or retrospective studies. On the other hand, one should not accept new therapies when the evidence comes exclusively from patient registries or retrospective data, since these types of studies are subject to biases and flaws.

One should be aware that most therapies in current clinical use are not supported by high level science.

Although the clinical practice guidelines present the best available evidence for clinical practice, not all guideline recommendations are based on the highest level of evidence, which is multiple randomized trials. Even in cardiology, which is one of the fields with the most extensive scientific documentation, many of the commonly used therapies are not documented with the highest level of evidence (Fanaroff et al., 2019). Therefore, in many cases, guideline recommendations are based on relatively weak data and on opinions of experts in the field, rather than on science. This is something we have to accept, and one cannot without good reason, stop using medicines when they have good therapeutic rationale, appear safe and there is no alternative. In some cases, it may be unethical to validate against the alternatives, and in other cases, there is not enough financial interest in the therapy to attract investors who will finance the testing. A properly designed study may cost millions of euros. When it comes to novel therapies, however, the general rule should be not to prescribe unless efficiency and safety is confirmed in randomized controlled trials.

In some Western countries, governments enforce financial restrictions which limit access to novel life-saving drugs which are already approved for use within the USA or European Union. As hospital leader, it is important to have systems which can help patients with getting access to such drugs when there is no other alternatives, such as in deadly cancer. There are currently rapid developments within personalized medicine, and it is not fair or humane that patients are denied or have delayed access to life-saving medicines which are already approved by health authorities in the USA and European Union. In some cases, the patients want to cover the expenses themselves which of course should be respected, although financing by government or health insurance would be better.

Usually, access to drugs which are not yet approved by the Food and Drug Administration or the European Medical Agency, so-called investigational drugs, is by participation in a clinical trial. There are, however, practical and medical reasons why some patients are not able to participate in clinical trials. Therefore, health authorities may allow companies to provide their experimental drugs to patients outside clinical trials. This is named *compassionate drug use*. In this way, unapproved drugs are made available to treat seriously ill patients when no other treatments are available. Each country has its own processes for getting access to drugs on these conditions. Patients should be made aware that such drugs have not been through all obligatory tests of safety and efficiency, and therefore it is not clear that they are beneficial. As hospital leader, it is important to have a system in place for how to handle such requests from patients.

An issue that is frequently discussed is a treatment option named "off-label." This is prescription of a drug that is already in clinical use, and is approved for one diagnosis, but not for a specific patient's disease or condition, and therefore not in accordance with the authorized product information. Whether or not to accept "off-label" use is both a medical issue and a question about reimbursement.

## 5.19   New Expensive Technology: A Case for Bundled Payment?

Over the last several years, there has been a revolutionary development in mini-invasive surgery and interventions, but the devices often are extremely expensive. One example is heart surgery, where heart valves can be replaced or repaired using a thin plastic tube introduced via a small artery on the leg, and is moved towards the hearts inside the blood vessel rather than by opening the chest. With this new so-called mini-invasive technique, patients have a faster recovery and fewer complications than with traditional surgery. The patients may spend less than 2 days in hospital instead of 2 weeks, and recover in less than 2 weeks instead of up to 2 months. The cost for the hospital of this new valve, however, is about ten times a traditional heart valve, but for society, the cost is no higher or even lower than with open heart surgery due to much shorter hospital stay, less time for recovery and fewer costly complications. Because most financing models do not consider total cost, the introduction of new cost-efficient therapies may be halted or slowed. In most hospitals, budgets only incorporate cost imposed inside the hospital, and therefore new treatment such as the mini-invasive heart valve surgery, may erroneously be considered a financial loss. This type of new innovation, and there are many others, could be cases for financing by bundled payment as discussed in Sect. 5.5.

## 5.20   A Leader Has Total Responsibility

In some hospitals, they separate between medical and financial leadership, which I discourage. If you lead only the medical part, you are a medical expert or a program director, but not a leader.

> In hospitals, a leader is accountable not only for the medical result, but for the total result, including finances.

In my experience, the most efficient organizational model is when all leaders at division, department, and section levels have total responsibility for results in their unit. This includes responsibility for clinical results, budget, manpower and the well-being of the employees. This model makes it clear who is responsible, and in a hospital this is essential.

The somewhat old-fashioned model where a medical doctor is clinical leader without responsibility for financial result is not sustainable and is not recommended.

## 5.21   Best Practice Budget Process

**Step 1: Define Strategy** At division level, the first step in the budget process is to define the strategic plan for the next budget year (Fig. 5.9). This strategy meeting should focus on defining next year's clinical activities, research and development and not primarily on budget. The way I do it, I request all leaders at all levels in the division to participate at this meeting. In addition, the administrative staff is present. Such wide representation secures that every leader gets a chance to give input.

**Fig. 5.9** Strategy meeting: This is the first step in budget preparation. All leaders at all levels in the division participate. Copyright: Otto A. Smiseth

**Step 2: Section Heads Propose Budget** In an organization with divisions, departments, and sections, each one of these units have their own internal process to define level of activity and the budgetary needs. The section leaders are key stakeholders in this process since they work directly with the patients and have the best insights into which activity is expected and wanted and the associated cost. They also have insights into new trends and treatments which may need to be incorporated in the budget. Importantly, in the early phase of the process, the section heads are not told what is their final budget; they are asked by the department head to propose the budget for their unit. This includes proposals for clinical activity, material expenses and number of employees needed. Furthermore, they are requested to come up with a proposal for how to improve efficiency. This process gives the section heads direct ownership to the budget and this strengthens budget loyalty. Of course not everything which is proposed may be accepted by their superior. The department head summarizes the budget proposals from the sections, adjusts when needed, and presents the department budget to the division head for discussion and approval.

**Step 3: Construction of Division Budget** The division head finalizes the budget proposal after a dialogue with each of the department heads. I recommend having 2–3 dedicated budget meetings with all the leaders in the division present. At these meetings, each department head presents their budget proposal. Departments that have not responded adequately to the budget claims will be exposed and get feedback from other leaders. The division head together with the finance manager finalizes the budget proposal and makes it ready for presentation to the hospital director.

**Step 4: The Budget Proposal from the Division Is Presented to the Hospital Director** A normal process is that the hospital director makes comments or requests changes in the budget. In the latter cases, the budget proposals are brought back to the department heads. As explained in this paragraph, involvement of leaders at all levels in the organization is recommended as this gives local leaders ownership to the budget. In this process, not everybody will agree, and usually not all proposals are taken into account, but people who are properly involved feel respected and become more motivated to contribute to reach the financial targets in the budget.

Involvement of all leaders in the budget process creates ownership to the budget which is critical for budget loyalty.

An important part of the budget process is to do a systematic risk assessment of the measures that are in the budget proposal. This includes a number of factors such as the market situation, staffing, and work load. If high risk is identified, measures should be taken to reduce the risk.

The budget process is like a stress test for all leaders, and differences in leader performance become more apparent. Since the budget defines the funding which is available for a unit, and the leader of the unit has accepted it during the budget process, it is by definition, always correct.

The budget is always correct!

It is fundamental for a sound organization that every leader accepts the budget for their unit. Within a budget year, a leader should never express to the employees that the budget is too small. In the process, before the budget is decided, it is of course fine to express views on the budget.

In some countries, there is tradition that unions are involved in the budget planning. If they are invited to take part in the process, the expectation should be that they contribute with proposals for how to improve productivity and the financial result. Of course, they are free to express opinions about what they do not like with the budget or what their concerns are, but that is not enough.

I discuss with the patient representatives when there are budget changes that will modify services significantly. Furthermore, I always invite a couple of representatives for the patient organizations to attend the budget conferences. They have always been constructive.

## 5.22    Manager Profiles and Budget

Over the years, I have been working in hospitals and medical organizations in many different countries and cultures and got to know many different leaders. For several years I served on the Board of the European Society of Cardiology, including a term as Treasurer, and met regularly with board members who were leaders at the main hospitals in Europe. We also had collaboration with several great clinical leaders from the USA. With regard to leadership style and budget attitude, there were almost unbelievable individual differences. None of the following are real people, but each profile is inspired by leaders I have personally met.

– *The excellent performer:* This department head always starts the budget process a few months prior to the anticipated starting point for hospital budgeting. Therefore, when the budget claims come from the hospital director, he already has prepared his team. He makes sure that each one of the section heads is involved in the budget planning, and is asked to come up with proposals for how to respond to the claims from the hospital director.

This department head has over the last several years recruited a couple of new section heads who share his philosophy about management. This excellent team knows that they must be up to speed in November or at least in December to have full effects of the measures in the budget from the first month of the next budget year. He has observed how departments which make budget plans at the end of the year, are delayed several months before their budget plans are fully implemented. Therefore, they face negative financial results in the first few months of the year, and to pick up the accumulated deficits, they need even more drastic measures to gain financial balance.

– *The pretender:* This department head pretends being loyal when meeting one-on-one with her superior, who is the division head, and verbally accepts the claims in the budget. However, she does not really care about staying on budget. Almost every year, her financial result is negative, but in this hospital organization, it has no consequence for her position. She considers her duty to be to deliver good medical services, whereas budget should be taken care of by the "finance people." Other departments in the same division are aware of this non-chalance, and it damages budget morale in these departments as well. The bad attitude of the department head is reflected in communication with her employees and therefore, the budget morale is not very good in this department. The hospital director is aware of the problem, which is not unique for this department, but he does not want to take the fights. This is because these departments provide critical surgical services, and he is afraid that patients may suffer if he demands stricter budget control.

- *The charismatic pacesetter:* Sometimes in medicine, exceptionally clever doctors who are highly respected by their colleagues, but with no real interest in management, float up to the top and become department heads. One of these is a famous, hard-working surgeon with a strong and charismatic personality. He is very outspoken, and expresses that all he needs is the resources to do the job, and he expects the hospital director to give him the resources he needs. He also seriously means and argues that you can fire most of the hospital administration since they just complicate life for the clinical workers. Because this leader is a powerful influencer and has very high work morale, he stimulates other surgeons to work hard as well. He does, however, create lots of frustration upstream in the line of command. What makes his department so good is also that he has attracted some of the best nurse leaders in town who coordinate patient admissions and manage the wards and operating rooms exceptionally well. He gives these nurse leaders the credit and attention they deserve.
- *Eager to please with no impact:* This personality is often selected as leaders since they are friendly and nice to work with for their superior. This leader honestly accepts everything coming from his superior and accepts the toughest budget claims. When it comes to executing decisions, however, he has a problem. He does not have the ability to enforce changes that are necessary because he is unable to face opposition. He therefore gets very little done.
- *The hidden jewel:* These are talented leaders who are not acknowledged for their positive contributions due to unprofessional management by their superiors. A typical case is a nurse who is head of a ward, which is a unit where the beds are located. Her superior, which is the

department head, is a medical doctor. He has advanced to become department head due to a combination of high medical competence and support from several other doctors, but his track record as leader is very slim. This nurse, similar to many other nurse leaders, has good management training. What is awkward in this case, is that this nurse who is a talented leader, has an amateur as boss. When she wants to discuss management issues, her leader is not able to support or advise her.

This nurse leader is well liked by the employees, and surveys indicate that the patients are satisfied. Her leader lacks insight into metrics, and is therefore not able to see how well this leader and her ward contribute to the clinical activity in the department. Furthermore, he does not appreciate all the work her team is doing with information and teaching of patients.

There are many talented nurse leaders out there who are working in an unprofessional organization which does not appreciate the work they are doing.

– *The dedicated worker:* This leader is head of a large clinical department and is an impressively hard worker, starting in his office at 6 am and continues until 8 pm or later. He has help from three different secretaries who take shifts, with the first starting when the leader arrives early in the morning. This leader works on research articles for the first one or two hours in the morning and does his own medical practice in the evening. In the middle of the day, he meets lots of people and other leaders. I spoke to one of the younger medical doctors working in this department, and he was very happy to work for this boss. He told me the boss knew the names of the children of all the doctors, and when they meet in the hallway, he may ask how his family is doing. This leader is a star in his field and attracts the best medical doctors. Patients from all over the country want referral to this department and also a number of international patients are referred. This hospital and in particular the department of this leader is listed among the very best in the annual ratings of US hospitals. The financial issues are taken care of by the section heads with support from a superb finance team. Due to lots of patient referrals, activity is high and the financial result is always good. Due to its high standing, this department also brings in lots of research funding which is like a magnet on the best doctors and nurses. The positive financial result of this department is in part used to support other departments when they are in trouble.

- *Fear-based leader:* A department leader from one of the European hospitals told me a surprising story about leadership by fear. He was in continuous financial deficit, and complained to me that his doctors had little interest in budget issues. One day at lunch, his secretary told him that she was aware that the doctors were talking negatively about the way he was leading the department. What he did then was to ask the secretary to summon all the medical doctors immediately in his office. They were asked to terminate all procedures as soon as possible. They all came to his office, and he gave them collectively a reprimand for the alleged slander.

  This leader told me that every now and then he had to scare his medical doctors to get control. I was surprised to hear that this type of leadership still exists. It was obviously not very efficient.

- *The dysfunctional and disloyal chair of the hospital board:* Loyalty goes both ways in an organization, which means the employees should be loyal to the leaders and vice versa.

  In a large hospital in one of the Southern European countries, there was a new chair of the hospital board who was hired to bring finances under control. At a hospital board meeting, he did something which should not happen in a professional organization. He demanded that all the division heads were present, and, in front of the hospital director, he openly criticized those division heads who had financial deficits, and asked them to bring finances under control. This of course was inappropriate as he set the hospital director aside.

  Furthermore, this chair of the hospital board wanted to please the government, which claimed that leaders in the health sector made too much money. During an interview on national TV, he attacked the clinical leaders in his own hospital and argued that they made too much money. Such disloyalty at the top is demoralizing for the entire organization.

  Leaders on the top of the hospital organization, including hospital director and the chair of the hospital board, should talk positively about subordinate leaders and employees, and use every occasion to make them shine.

## 5.23   Have Responsibility Centers: Avoid Cost Centers

A *cost center* is an organizational unit where the leader is accountable only for expenses, but not directly responsible for revenues. Units such as IT, accounting, and human resources are often organized as cost centers, which is fine since they have no direct revenues unless there is internal invoicing. The alternative model is *responsibility center* which means that the leader is responsible for both cost and revenue.

The largest clinical units, the divisions and departments are usually responsibility centers, whereas the smaller clinical units (sections) are often cost centers. Most of the clinical decisions in a hospital are taken at the section level. This implies that the section level is the most important control point for regulating financial result and efficiency. Therefore, it is a weakness in a hospital organization when the clinical sections are cost centers.

There will be a tendency that cost centers solve financial problems by reducing activity, which means helping fewer patients, whereas responsibility centers can solve the problem by increasing activity, thus generating more revenue and helping more patients. My recommendation is that all revenue generating units are organized as responsibility centers. This means that the leaders are accountable for both expenses and revenues.

Figure 5.10 illustrates how cost centers can weaken productivity. In this case, the department is a responsibility center and the sections, the ward and the heart laboratory, are cost centers. The *ward* is where the hospital beds are located, and where patients stay prior to and after interventions at the *heart laboratory*. In the case shown in Fig. 5.10, the section heads are happy with their financial result since cost is according to the budget and even slightly less. They are not worried about the activity, which is a little low, but revenues are not part of their financial responsibility. Furthermore, if waiting times for admission should go up, there is good capacity in other hospitals in town. Therefore, they are confident that the patients do not suffer even though the department head seems to have problems with the economy.

The department head is not happy since his financial result, which is determined by both cost and revenue, is negative. This is because the clinical activity at the sections is below budget and therefore the DRG-based revenue is low.

The organization in Fig. 5.10 can easily be changed to responsibility centers at the sections as well. At the heart laboratory, this is easy since every procedure has a defined price. The ward could get a fraction of the price since they also contribute to the patient care. This way the head of the ward would have a financial incentive to increase activity and utilize available beds better.

It has been argued that making clinical units into responsibility centers is complicated. If the ambition is to have 100% accuracy on revenues, it

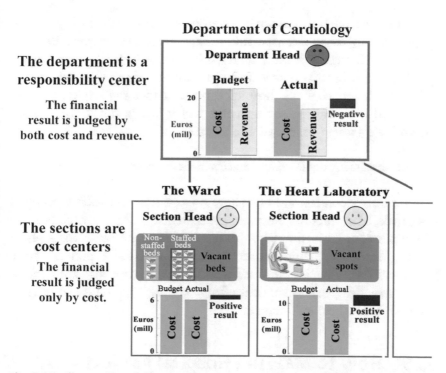

**Fig. 5.10** Illustration of department as responsibility center and sections as cost centers. The section heads have positive results and are happy. The department head, however, has a negative result because the activity-based revenues at the sections are below plan. The section heads have no financial incentive to fill up vacant beds at the ward and use available slots in the heart laboratory. Copyright: Otto A. Smiseth

is complicated, but there is no reason to have perfect accuracy. The point is that focus on both revenue and cost will improve productivity.

The same problem is seen when service departments, like radiology or anaesthesiology, are cost centers and the clinical departments are responsibility centers. This can be changed by making at least part of their budget activity based.

## 5.24 Running Hospital Means Running Business

Hospitals are large businesses with often several thousand employees, and operating budgets are comparable to medium-sized or large industry companies. Therefore, leaders at all levels need to have the business perspective as part of their management philosophy. If not, the patients will ultimately suffer when the hospital cannot finance the services needed. Importantly, the patient should never feel it is a business. The leaders should have a warm heart and a cool brain.

Avoid that financing influences single patient decisions.

Since most doctors and nurses have no or limited business training, it is essential that there is business competence in the central hospital administration. Unfortunately, this is not always the case. It is a severe problem having a finance director with no practical experience from business. When that is combined with clinical leaders who for obvious reasons usually have no experience from business, the result can be catastrophic for the hospital finances.

## 5.25 How to Measure Hospital Productivity?

Productivity is traditionally measured as the output per unit of input. In industries, the output can be measured as the ratio between number of units produced, of a defined standard, and the cost of the production. Measuring productivity for a hospital, however, is complicated due to the large number of different medical conditions represented and the unprecise definition of "the product." The definition should include standards for the quality of the product, which is hard to measure. There are exceptions, however, such as hip replacements, cataract surgeries and several other standardized procedures. For most hospital procedures, however, the "product" is not standardized due to differences in patient complexity.

When a department is comparing productivity over time and the case mix is relatively stable, productivity can be calculated as cost per treated patient. If you want to do a comparison of your own productivity with that of other hospitals, it becomes more complicated since it is difficult to get the information needed to make accurate comparisons.

In countries with DRG-based financing, the cost per DRG produced may be used as an index of productivity. With regard to efficiency of the manpower, one can calculate productivity as number of employees per DRG. Since in principle, one DRG reflects the cost of treating one patient, the number of employees divided with the number of DRG points produced, reflects efficiency. Importantly, this method should not be used to compare efficiency between different medical specialties in the hospital because DRG also reflects cost of technologies and not only manpower. As an example, neurosurgery uses some very expensive implants, which explains high DRG for neurosurgical procedures. In contrast, general internal medicine, which uses more low-cost technologies, produces much less DRG. Therefore, one should not use number of employees needed to produce one DRG to compare efficiency between the department of neurosurgery and department of internal medicine. On the other hand, number of employees per DRG can be used to compare neurosurgery departments at different hospitals provided they treat essentially similar patients.

## 5.26   Optimize the Number of Nurses

Without comparison, the biggest financial challenge for hospitals is controlling the number of employees. As illustrated by the OECD data presented in Sect. 5.1, the number of health workers is steadily rising, and in some countries appear to be out of control. Although individual medical doctors have the highest salaries, the largest payroll cost is to nurses because they by far exceed the number of doctors. Therefore, optimizing the number of nurses must be high on the agenda for all hospital leaders.

There are several drivers behind the ongoing increase in number of nurses in hospitals. This includes aging of the population and medical innovations, which implies that more people live a long life with chronic illnesses. Furthermore, governmental regulations regarding working time and standards of work environment increases need for staffing. Finally, laws and regulations regarding patient safety have implications on staffing needs. These drivers for increase in hospital staffing represent positive changes which the society wants.

The two main strategies for improving efficiency and optimizing the number of nurses are (1) reduction in the number of hospital beds by shortening the length of stay and more use of outpatient care and hotels, and (2) efficient use of the capacity of nurses by optimal planning and coordination. These issues are discussed in Sect. 5.16.

An opportunity to downsize the number of hospital employees is when plans are made for new hospital buildings. Discussions about hospital size are often brought to the media, and the discussions can be very heated. The organizations representing nurses and doctors, typically argue in favor of making the hospital bigger with more beds, since that is what they consider is needed. The elephant in the room is the number of nurses, which will increase proportionally with the number of beds and lead to an increase in the annual cost of running the hospital. This is the most important reason for being restrictive with number of beds when planning new hospitals. There is of course a larger investment cost when making the building larger, but long-term it is the salaries which represent the largest financial challenge.

> Patients often stay too long in hospitals—this is not good for health and bad for economy.

In medical departments, it is almost like a reflex that when a hospital bed is available, it is filled with patients, which means extra nursing cost. Why does it happen and why is it so difficult to reduce the number of hospital beds? There are several reasons why hospital beds tend to fill up regardless of bed capacity, but few of these are in the best interest of the health of the patients. Staying in hospital too long is bad for health due to risk of blood clots due to inactivity and infections with dangerous hospital bacteria.

If a patient needs extended medical care or repeated medical contact, use hotel and outpatient care.

When you are in a health crisis as during the Covid-19 pandemic, what matters is the competence of the nurses, not just the number. The most critical capacity limitation during the pandemic was the number of intensive care nurses. These nurses have been through extensive qualification programs, which include practice with the most severely ill patients. They are used to handle dramatic situations such as traumatic injuries, acute medical conditions of any sort and complications after surgery.

Make sure you plan for crises by having adequate staffing of intensive care nurses. This was an important lesson from the Covid-19 pandemic.

The work intensive care nurses do with critically sick children and adults is mentally demanding, and they often have exhausting work schedules which include frequent night shifts and weekends. To recruit and keep these "super-nurses," give them as flexible working conditions as you can and pay them well. In my division, I meet the leaders of the intensive care and intermediate care units every morning at the "whiteboard meetings" (Sect. 4.5) to discuss capacity and support them. The intensive care nurses are often times criticized because capacity is limited for reasons beyond their control. This is not appropriate for nurses who do their best to help the sickest of the sick patients.

It is important for clinical leaders and hospital directors to ensure adequate staffing with intensive care nurses.

When intensive care nurses want a break from their demanding job, they are well suited for other positions in the hospital. Since they can manage any acute event, everybody appreciates having an intensive care qualified nurse in the team. When during a flight, the stewardess announces "is there a doctor on board" it would be better to announce "is there a doctor or intensive care nurse on board" since the latter usually does better than most doctors when there is a cardiac arrest.

An important lesson from the Covid-19 pandemic was that capacity of health care was insufficient to meet the medical needs of the large number of infected patients. In particular, the number of intensive care nurses was insufficient. It is expected that society makes preparations for managing future health crises similar to the Covid-19 pandemic. This includes making plans for higher reserve capacity for intensive care. The cost of the increased capacity will come on top of the financial burden which health care represents to day, and may not be sustainable unless the efficiency of the services is improved. In my opinion, this requires research into how the workload on nurses and physicians can be reduced by more use of nurse assistants and physician assistants as a cheaper workforce. There are many practical tasks done by the nurses and doctors which do not require high-level nursing or medical competence. Unfortunately, there are legal barriers, which slow down or prevent such a transition. The professional organizations and regulatory authorities should look into this issue and establish systems for how to make transition of tasks to assistants safe and compatible with good standards of care.

Another important change to consider is to stratify nursing competence at different levels instead of just two levels. In addition to the levels of competence typically in use today, with the majority of nurses having general nursing training and working at the wards, and highly specialized nurses working at intensive care units, one should have nurses trained for intermediate levels of care. That is nurses who are trained to take care of patients who are too complex to be at the general wards, but do not need ventilators or complex cardiorespiratory support systems. In my division there was always a number of intermediate care beds, which allowed much less staffing than for intensive care. Importantly, intermediate level of care does not mean lower quality of care, but staffing is matched to the needs of less complex patients at these units. In this way, substantially larger volumes of patients can be taken care of by the same total number of nurses. It should be looked into if this intermediate level of care may be used more extensively during pandemics and other large-scale health crises. Sufficient training for the intermediate care nurses can be maintained by having them work temporarily a few weeks a year at the intensive care units.

Furthermore, as was done in the UK during the last pandemic, the military can be mobilized to assist the health workers with administration of vaccines or other tasks. One should consider if the armed forces can be prepared to play an even more important role in health crises in the future. Since crises such as during the Covid-19 pandemic are just intermittent, it is not a sustainable solution to scale up permanent positions to a level which may or may not be needed in a future crisis. Rather than planning permanent overcapacity, one should plan for systems which allow rapid mobilization of extra personnel.

When planning new hospitals, it is important to consider solutions for temporary increase in bed capacity, since health crises can last for several months and years, as seen with the Covid-19 pandemic. It is not acceptable with extended periods with reduced basic hospital activity, resulting in too long waiting times for patients with cancer or other deadly or disabling diseases. One option is to expand the hospital hotel capacity and use this in a flexible manner. When more capacity is needed, hotel beds may be converted to regular hospital beds. Having patients in their home, combined with close follow up from hospitals was used during the Covid-19 pandemic. Hospitals-at-home programs have been practiced for several years, and novel technologies for distant biometric monitoring and video visits have increased the feasibility of this type of care. The hospital-at-home model may be applied for many different medical conditions. There is need for more research into how hospital-at-home care can be expanded in a way which is more cost efficient than traditional hospital care, and with no compromises on safety and medical quality.

## 5.27  Management and Financial Crisis

When the hospital gets financial problems in the middle of a budget year, it puts lots of stress on the leaders. Typically, the chair of the hospital board calls for a crisis meeting with the hospital director who is asked to come up with corrective action. He summons a meeting with the division or department heads and asks for corrective action, and similar action is requested from leaders further down in the organization. The easiest way out is to increase revenues, which is often feasible in hospitals which are financed by fee for service (DRG-based financing or other models). The other obligatory consideration is to reduce expenses. Since 50–70% of hospital expenses are salaries, reducing personnel cost is often needed to bring the finances in balance.

Now you can harvest from the investment you made in seeing your people, supporting them and showing respect. This has made the employees more motivated to listen to you and follow you as a leader when there is crisis. If you show no interest in the employees and their work when they are struggling, it is less likely that they will care for you when you have a problem.

During a crisis, it is more important than ever to have your walking tours and spend time with your employees. If the walking around tour in the clinical units takes 2–4 hours a week, it is time well spent. To get time, just reduce the duration of administrative meetings.

## 5.28   Avoid Outsourcing to Monopolies

Outsourcing hospital services can be good provided you can get the same or better quality on the service and at lower price. When there is only one company with competence to take on the outsourced activity, which means monopoly, services tend to become worse. In my experience it also becomes more expensive since there is no competition. Companies with monopoly tend to start living their own life and care too much for their own well-being and too little for the patients. I have seen bad cases where this happened. Therefore, unless you are convinced there is real competition, it is better not to outsource. Having the service from a department inside the hospital means you can more easily give direct feedback to the service provider.

## 5.29    Use Consultant Companies Only if You Know Where to Go

Hospitals waste incredible amounts of money on hiring consultant companies. I have seen 10s of millions of euros wasted on hiring consultant companies. A main reason for the waste was that the hospital manager did not know what should be obtained other than general goals like improvement of efficiency. If you do not see a solution, do not expect that a non-medical business organization can help you.

The recipe for success is first, that you and your team, including leaders working on the floor, have decided where you want to go, but need help to get there. If you do not know where you want to go, there is little chance that a consultant company can help you. Furthermore, your goals should be numerical, and make a plan for when and how to evaluate the results.

Importantly, if you do things right, hiring a consultant company can give you and your employees an uplifting, which is hard to get with a sleepy or solidified organization. When you and your team know where you want to go, when the consultant company provides their best people, and when the personal chemistry between your team and the consultants is good, you can achieve great results. In one of my first leader position, this happened and gave my department a boost which lasted for many years. Stimulated by our results, another hospital hired the same consultant company, but then essentially nothing was achieved since they had no idea about what they wanted to achieve other than nonspecific objectives such as improvement of efficiency and quality.

# References

Agarwal, R., Liao, J. M., Gupta, A., & Navathe, A. S. (2020). The impact of bundled payment on health care spending, utilization, and quality: A systematic review. *Health Aff (Millwood), 39*(1), 50–57.

Al Talalwah, N., & McIltrot, K. H. (2019, Feb). Cancellation of surgeries: Integrative review. *Journal of PeriAnesthesia Nursing, 34*(1), 86–96.

Anderson, G. F., Hussey P., & Petrosyan, V. (2019, Jan). It's still the prices, stupid: Why the US spends so much on health care, and a tribute to uwe reinhardt. *Health Aff (Millwood)*, *38*(1), 87–95.

Anderson, G. F., Reinhardt, U. E., Hussey, P. S., & Petrosyan, V. (2003, May–Jun). It's the prices, stupid: Why the United States is so different from other countries. *Health Aff (Millwood)*, *22*(3), 89–105.

Deloitte. (2017) *Survey of US health system CEOs: Moving forward in an uncertain environment*. The Deloitte Center for Health Solutions.

Edwards, N., & Marshall, M. (2003). Doctors and managers. *BMJ*, *326*(7381), 116–117.

Fanaroff, A. C., Califf, R. M., Windecker, S., Smith, S. C., Jr., & Lopes, R. D. (2019, Mar 19). Levels of Evidence Supporting American College of Cardiology/American Heart Association and European Society of Cardiology Guidelines, 2008–2018. *JAMA*, *321*(11), 1069–1080.

Hemmings, P., & Prinz, C. (2020). Sickness and disability systems: Comparing outcomes and policies in Norway with those in Sweden, the Netherlands and Switzerland. *OECD Economics Department Working Papers*, 2020, No. 1601, OECD Publishing, Paris, https://doi.org/10.1787/c768699b-en.

Levitt, T. (1960). Marketing Myopia. *Harvard Business Review*.

Levitt, T. (2004). Marketing Myopia. *Harvard Business Review – Classics*.

Lyu, H., Xu, T., Brotman, D., Mayer-Blackwell, B., Cooper, M., Daniel, M., Wick, E. C., Saini, V., Brownlee, S., & Makary, M. A. (2017, Sep 6). Overtreatment in the United States. *PLoS One*. *12*(9).

OECD, Health at a Glance 2019: *OECD Indicators*. OECD Publishing, Paris. https://doi.org/10.1787/4dd50c09-en.

Park, J., et al. (2019, May 7). KAMIR-NIH (Korea Acute Myocardial Infarction Registry–National Institutes of Health) investigators. Prognostic implications of door-to-balloon time and onset-to-door time on mortality in patients with ST-segment-elevation myocardial infarction treated with primary percutaneous coronary intervention. *Journal of the American Heart Association*, *8*(9), e012188. https://doi.org/10.1161/JAHA.119.012188. PMID: 31041869; PMCID: PMC6512115.

TEConomy Partners, LLC. (2019, December). *The economic impact of the US biopharmaceutical Industry: 2017 National and State estimates*.

# 6

# How to Make Decisions

**Abstract** Making decisions and taking action is what leadership is all about. Therefore, the quality of decision processes is critical to your success as leader. In knowledge organizations such as hospitals, a process with several steps is needed before a decision is valid.

When making big decisions with irreversible or long-term effects, one should be aware of the risk of biases which may lead to suboptimal or even wrong decisions. First, make sure that alternative solutions are fully explored, independently from the decision makers. Second, ask yourself if the decision makers have fallen in love with their own solution, and therefore are blind for its weaknesses. Third, unanimous decisions on complex issues may suggest that decision makers have degenerated into group think. Fourth, be careful when consulting companies are involved as their own interest, such as hope for future contracts, acts like a momentum, which drives the process forward.

Compassionate leadership is about showing empathy and respect when you interact with employees. The chapter explains the method of compassionate leadership, which is more efficient than just telling employees what to do.

© The Author(s), under exclusive license to Springer Nature Switzerland AG 2023  **101**
O. A. Smiseth, *Managing a Hospital*, Business Guides on the Go,
https://doi.org/10.1007/978-3-031-17611-1_6

This chapter describes the World Café method as an excellent way to secure good involvement when making decisions.

## 6.1 The Art of Making Decisions

What is a decision? When a boss comes back from a holiday with a new idea and announces that he has decided to change the way the department is organized, this is not a valid decision. At the best, it is a good idea, but nothing more. In an organization such as a hospital or any knowledge organization, several steps are needed before a decision is valid. This is illustrated in Fig. 6.1. Of course, decisions regarding individual patients and operative issues are taken several times every day, but now we are discussing decisions which will change the way people work.

In the following, we will discuss decisions made at department level, but the principles are similar at any level in the organization. Before you as department head propose something for decision, it is essential to check that what you propose is feasible within the current buildings and infrastructure and is not in conflict with the responsibilities of the hospital.

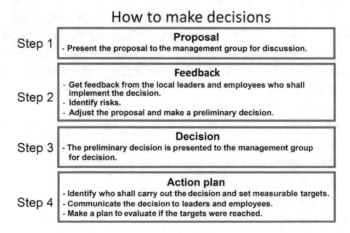

**Fig. 6.1** Critical steps for making good decisions: A successful decision requires that all steps are taken care of. Copyright: Otto A. Smiseth

As a quality control before you propose the decision, get the opinion of a couple of trusted and smart people who know the field well. This should include consideration of potential unacceptable risks associated with your proposal. If there are, you may decide not to proceed. Furthermore, make sure that the local leader who will be most involved is consulted, and he needs to agree on the proposed change. If he does not agree, the proposal is not ready for presentation to the management group.

Always involve your superior, which in this case is the division head. Furthermore, when the change will influence other divisions, the hospital director should be informed just to be prepared in case the other divisions are complaining or asking what is going on. When the proposed change includes substantial investment in infrastructure, the proposal usually needs to be presented to the hospital director or the hospital board or both for approval.

To make decisions, the following procedure is recommended:

Step 1—Discuss the proposal in your management group: You get comments from the group and adjust the proposal accordingly. Then you move to the next step.

Step 2—Get feedback from local leaders and the employees and make a preliminary decision: The way employees are involved in making decisions varies widely between countries and cultures. In some countries, there are laws and regulations about work environment which makes it obligatory to involve the workers. The apparently quick and easy way is to announce that a decision has been made, and then go ahead. For many simple issues, this is just fine. For more comprehensive changes, involvement of employees is highly recommended.

In my experience, when employees are involved in the decision process and support the change, it will facilitate implementation. In cases where the employees disagree, it is of course you as leader who decide. It is always nice when people agree with you, but you should also appreciate and listen to people who disagree. The opinions of those who disagree may be the most important feedback you get. The World Café method, which is explained in Sect. 6.3, is recommended as an efficient way of getting feedback from other leaders as well as employees.

Step 3—Decision: After having considered the feedback from the local leaders and the employees, you present the adjusted proposal to the management group of the department for final decision. This is done along with presentation of a risk analysis when that is needed. If important risks are identified, you take measures to reduce risk while moving ahead.

Step 4—Action plan: Identify the persons who shall carry out the change and set a deadline for implementation. In every action plan, there should be a target in terms of financial and/or quality improvement. In either case, the target should be objective and feasible to measure. The decision and action plan are then communicated via the local leaders, sometimes supplemented with a newsletter or an open information meeting.

Always evaluate results from major decisions and if results were not achieved, make necessary adjustments.

For decisions which result in large changes, it may be useful to have a steering group to monitor progress. I recommend having no more than four to five people in the steering group. If the group is large, it tends to become inefficient. Before final decisions are taken, do a quality check on the decision process, including a check for biases, and make sure that comments from the employees are considered.

By following this 4 steps procedure, all stakeholders in the decision have been involved. When other divisions are heavily influenced, they should be consulted before a final decision is made. If not consulted, they may run to the hospital director and complain, and you may not be allowed to make the change you want.

Unless all 4 steps are taken care of, there is not a valid decision. Quite often only the first one or two steps are taken care of, and then often nothing happens other than creation of frustration in the management and loss of credibility for the leader.

There is not much work with this process for making decisions. It takes no more than a few weeks to get through all steps and unless unexpected conflicts arise, only a few meetings are needed. If involvement is not done properly, there is often a lot of friction which consumes time and causes delay.

Making decisions and taking action is what leadership is all about. Therefore, the quality of decision processes is critical to your success as leader.

## 6.1.1 The Big Decisions

Sometimes a hospital makes big decisions which have irreversible long-term effects on the structure of the hospital, such as hospital mergers or major organizational changes. In a busy hospital, the leaders and employees may be overruled by big decisions made at the hospital board or higher levels. This is unfortunate since important feedback may be lost, and lack of process stimulates resistance against implementation of the decisions. What apparently was a quick and easy decision may end up as a disturbing conflict inside the organization.

When big decisions are taken, it is essential that the local leaders, who shall ultimately implement the decision, are involved. A Harvard Business Review article by David Kahneman et al. (2011) discusses and highlights important issues about quality control when taking big decisions. The subtitle of their article is *"Dangerous biases can creep into every strategic choice. Here's how to find them - before they lead you astray."* David Kahneman was awarded the Nobel Prize in Economic Sciences in 2002 for having integrated insights from psychological research into economic science, especially concerning human judgment and decision-making under uncertainty.

Figure 6.2 highlights some of the questions which should be asked before making big decisions. The first question is to ask if alternative solutions have been *fully explored*. Importantly, the people who will ultimately decide often have biases and should therefore not be allowed to interfere with the process of exploring alternative solutions. As stated in the article by Kahneman et al. (2011), "in a good decision process, other alternatives are fully evaluated in an objective and fact-based way."

The second question, if the team has *fallen in love* with its proposal, is also important. Falling in love with one particular proposal tends to make you blind for seeing its weaknesses.

**Before making Big Decisions, Ask yourself**

## 1
**Were alternative solutions fully explored?**

To avoid biases, those exploring alternatives should be completely independent from the decision makers

## 2
**Has the team fallen In love with its proposal?**

Love makes you blind for seeing negative sides of a proposal

## 3
**Is disagreement hidden in group think?**

Be suspicious when a team makes unanimous decisions about complex issues

**Fig. 6.2** Critical questions to ask when making Big Decisions: The topic is reviewed by Kahneman et al. (2011). Copyright: Otto A. Smiseth

The third question to be asked is whether disagreement in the group may be hidden in *group think* as a mechanism to minimize conflict. When a group degenerates into groupthink, there is increased risk of suboptimal or even irrational decisions.

As pointed out in the article by Kahneman et al. (2011), "an absence of dissent in a team addressing a complex problem, should sound an alarm." A unanimous decision in a management group could be "sham unity" imposed by the team's leader.

Furthermore, one should also be careful when decisions are based on extensive work from consultant companies or architects with self-interest in continuing the project. These companies may generate so much momentum in the project that change in direction or discussion of alternative solutions becomes very difficult. An open process with proper involvement of local leaders is the best protection against biases and defects in thinking. As stated by Kahneman et al. (2011), "Organizations need to realize that a disciplined decision-making process, not individual genius, is the key to a sound strategy."

Big decisions regarding hospital mergers and locations often generate lots of external attention, and the hospital owner may have to defend in the media why the proposed change is needed. A sign that one should consider to abandon a proposed solution is when nobody in town other than the consultant company working on the project, and high-level administrators who initiated the big change, consider it to be a good solution. It is important to remember that consultant companies often know little or nothing about medicine.

Unfortunately, boards and sometimes politicians consider it a sign of weakness to change a major decision. Therefore, apparently bad decisions are not reversed in time.

## 6.2   The Power of Compassionate Leadership

When approaching a problematic situation, where you understand that employees disagree with you, the following approach, which is named compassionate leadership, can be very helpful (Atkins & Parker, 2012; West et al., 2017). Jeff Weiner, CEO of LinkedIn, defines compassion as "empathy plus action."

*The principles of compassionate leadership* can be useful for many situations in life, not only at work. Essentials of compassionate leadership are listening to and showing empathy with the employees, which can create a shift from negative attitudes to positive creativity.

Compassionate leadership has four elements:

1. Start with paying attention to the employee: You should listen with fascination, not just listening. You clarify by asking questions, and you repeatedly summarize with one or two sentences to check if you got it right.

   It is more likely that the team members will make suggestions proactively when knowing their voices are listened to and their perspective is appreciated.
2. Next, find a shared understanding of the situation: When you appear to disagree, try to agree upon where you truly disagree. Importantly, show respect.
3. Show empathy when discussing: Empathic leadership increases team member motivation and creativity.

4. Finally, decide and take intelligent action: Thoughtful and intelligent action that engages and involves the employees is more efficient than just telling them what to do. You do not need to agree with the employees in everything, but involving them will reduce resistance to changes.

*This 4 steps model can be used in many different situations to involve employees in making decisions.*

Since health care is under heavy financial pressure with increasing focus on metrics and productivity, compassion between leaders and employees and between health worker and patients is more important than ever. The principles of compassionate leadership can be applied systematically to build a culture which combines empathy and productivity.

## 6.3    World Café to Empower Decisions

The World Café method (http://theworldcafe.com) is recommended to anchor decisions with other leaders and employees. When applying the decision algorithm in Fig. 6.1, World Café is well suited during Step 2.

Figure 6.3 illustrates how the World Café method works. In this example, a department head wants feedback on his ideas for how to solve a problem. He has four different potential solutions. The session starts with an introduction by the department head of why a change is needed. The session typically lasts for 2–3 hours.

In the case illustrated in Fig. 6.3 there are six employees grouped around each table. This includes a table host who stays at the same table, while the other attendees rotate between tables to give their opinions about each of the solutions. The table host takes notes, and at the end of the session, all participants get together, and each host presents a brief summary from her/his table. Finally, the chair of the session, which in this case was the department head, has a presentation where he summarizes and makes a preliminary conclusive statement from the entire session. In some cases, the department head may want to further explore the

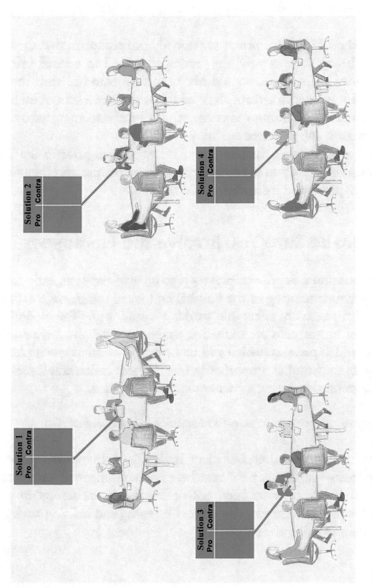

**Fig. 6.3** Illustration of World Café grouping around tables. Copyright: Otto A. Smiseth

preferred solution with regard to risks. Subsequently the preferred solution is presented to the management group for final decision (Step 3 in Fig. 6.1).

With the World Café procedure nobody can complain that their view was not heard. Importantly, the participants need to be well informed and listened to, and you should not use this method to rush through. Time is not wasted in writing detailed minutes since a scan of each table sheet can serve as minutes together with a brief document which concludes what is the preferred option.

It is important that the table hosts are appointed prior to the World Café meeting. Here you need some of your best people, and they need to be well prepared and instructed about their role.

## 6.4    Make Sure You Involve the Employees

The expectation from the employees is to be involved at an early stage in any larger restructuring of the hospital and when the management considers changes with effect on working conditions. The majority of employees in hospitals are trained at university level and have excellent insights and experience which will be helpful for leaders when planning changes in the hospital. Importantly, involvement makes employees more positive to implementing a change when it is decided.

Ability to run good processes is a hallmark of a good leader.

A hallmark of good and efficient leaders is ability to run good and open processes, and a key element here is involvement of employees in decisions. Please refer to Sect. 6.2 on *compassionate leadership* which highlights the importance of interested listening and holding back judgment when meeting the employees.

## 6.5    Dialogue with the Labor Unions

In most OECD countries, organized labor represents a relatively small fraction of the employees. The Scandinavian countries are an exception, as most employees are organized in unions.

To develop and maintain a professional relationship with the unions, it is essential that both parts are clear about their roles, and it requires that the employer gives priority to dialogue with the union leaders. As division head, I have regular meetings with the major union representatives all together once a month, and I also have face-to-face meeting with one union representative at a time if they want. These are great meeting where we often disagree, but build mutual confidence.

I also include the union representatives in the budget planning meetings. Importantly, my expectation to the unions is that they contribute with constructive feedback, not only negative. Furthermore, when they completely disagree with a solution proposed by the leader, they should come up with an alternative solution.

In the units that I personally have been managing, I had mostly excellent union representatives. There were a few exceptions, but that often reflected that they had local challenges.

There are reports from large hospital organizations of occasional union leaders who get lots of power and privileges, and tend to behave as "bosses," not only as advocates for the employees they are meant to support.

It is entirely legitimate that union leaders negotiate and put pressure on the hospital leaders to get better working conditions, higher salary and more staff. This is part of their duty on behalf of the employees they represent.

## 6.6    Formal and Informal Leadership

Importantly, the organizational charts in Figs. 4.1 and 4.2 only show formal relationships and tell nothing of the pattern of human (social) relationships which develop and which is important in any organization. Even in a hierarchical (vertical) organization, there are important relations which do not follow the lines of command and which are important for the daily operations.

## References

Atkins, P. W. B., & Parker, S. K. (2012). Understanding individual compassion in organizations: The role of appraisals and psychological flexibility. *The Academy of Management Review, 37*(4), 524–546.

Kahneman, D., Lovallo, D., & Sibony, O. (June 2011). Before you make that big decision... Dangerous biases can creep into every strategic choice. Here's how to find them – before they lead you astray. *Harvard Business Review, 89*, 50–60.

West, M., Eckert, R., Collins, B., & Chowla, R. (May 2017). *Caring to change. How compassionate leadership can stimulate innovation in health care.* The King's Fund.

# 7

# See Your Employees and Define Your Personal Added Value

**Abstract** When you become aware that your employees do something well, make sure you give them recognition. People who are seen by the leader will be much more motivated to help the leader when needed. Therefore, it is important for leaders to get out of their office, move around and see the employees when they are working. Use meetings to listen to and discuss with your subordinate leaders and employees, and to show them respect for the work they do. This also has a positive effect on the work environment.

As a clinical leader, you are an executive, which means you are a doer and should execute your plans. It is not enough to be a controller or solver of administrative problems. As leader, you should primarily be a developer with defined goals. Write an action plan for the next couple of years rather than for a more distant future since that will be less binding. Set your objectives for what shall be your personal contribution to the hospital.

Employee pulse surveys are anonymous questionnaires to all employees to measure how they see working conditions. The responses express organizational health and can identify problems, which the leader should take care of.

## 7.1    Be Fair and Show Respect

Leaders who treat their employees with respect and fairness will in the long run obtain the best results. Run open and good processes and make decisions that from both the inside of the organization and from the outside seem fair. People like to work with fair leaders who will then attract the best employees.

Fundamental to every human being is that they want to be respected. Use every occasion you have to show respect for your employees. This is also the best way for you to be respected.

It never fails, if you show respect, you get respect.

When you become aware that your employees do something well, make sure you give them recognition. Send a thanks for what they do for the patients, and put their local leader on copy. Your enthusiasm for excellence is contagious.

## 7.2    Celebrate Achievements

Give your employees attention and find occasions to celebrate achievements for individuals or teams.

It is well known that positive feedback strengthens motivation. In particular young people are stimulated by positive feedback and is an even more powerful stimulus than money and other benefits.

## 7.3    See Your Employees When They Work

Spend as much time as you can to meet and see your employees while they are working. Do it with a smile and ask what they are doing that day.

I happened to meet one of the IKEA center directors and discussed management with him. Since IKEA is one of the most successful businesses in the world, I asked what was special with their famous CEO, Ingvar Kamprad, and how he was able to achieve such results. Did he interact directly with his people or did he just sit on the top of the company and make strategic plans and collect the results? This center director told me that Mr. Kamprad liked to meet the people working for him and would regularly visit every IKEA store.

I asked the center director what Mr. Kamprad focused on the last time he made a visit to the store. Kamprad, as always, wanted to meet as early as possible in the morning, and they decided to meet in the warehouse since that was where employees came first. When they got there, the first employee had just arrived. When they approached him, Mr. Kamprad asked the center director silently what his name was. Fortunately, the director knew the name of the warehouseman, and Mr. Kamprad started to talk to him friendly about the work he was doing. Mr. Kamprad also wanted to meet the cashiers. When they approached the first cashier, Mr. Kamprad again asked the center director what her name was. Then he started to talk to her, and Mr. Kamprad discussed if some of the items could be placed differently on the shelf to be more visible for the customer.

The management lesson from this story is that you should meet your employees and show interest in the work they are doing. This will increase employee motivation. Another reason why Mr. Kamprad did this round was to test if the center director knew the names of his employees, as a sign that he was leading according to the philosophy of the IKEA company.

## 7.4 Listen More and Do It Right

When you conduct team meetings, do not talk too much. Let your team members do most of the talking. You start by raising a question, and you summarize intermittently during and at the end of the meeting. Try to listen more than you talk.

Make sure each member of the group feel they get your attention. You achieve that by establishing eye contact with each one of the team members while you are discussing. You should do that repeatedly during the meeting. Do not forget anybody, not even those who are quiet and usually say nothing. I learned this from a singer who explained how he used eye contact to become emotionally connected with the audience. He explained that when he was performing, he continuously shifted eye contact across the crowd so that everybody got the feeling that he looked at them.

Furthermore, never start meetings abruptly, tune in softly by talking about something neutral and nice, and do not forget to smile.

## 7.5    Define Your Hospital's Core Values

Define which values you will bring to the patients. These values, which the patients may have seen on the website of your hospital, should be the same as they experience when they are hospitalized. Do not make a long list of politically correct statements, but identify just the few most important ones which you want to have as your guide. When there are tough times and you need to reorganize or increase productivity, make sure you stick to these values.

## 7.6    Define Your Personal Added Value

You should define what will be your added value as leader. Therefore, set your personal objectives for what shall be your contributions to the hospital over the next couple of years.

Do not limit yourself to being a problem solver and controller. There may be times when you spend most of your energy on solving administrative problems or on financial control, but this is not sufficient contribution from a leader. You should also be a driver for developing the unit you are leading, and provide better services to the patients.

> For a clinical leader, it is not enough to be a problem solver and controller. You should primarily be a developer with defined goals.

As a clinical leader, you are an executive, which means you are a doer who should execute your plans. Involve your management group and employees and discuss with your key people where you want the hospital to go the coming years. Write an action plan for the next 2–3 years, rather than for more distant future since that will be less binding. Present your plan to your superior and get his support. Set objectives and part of the plan should be to check your results against the objectives.

Importantly, your added value is not something you achieve alone, but your action is needed to get it done. How this may work is illustrated by the following examples from my own hospital in position as clinical leader. It is important to note that the results were obtained by working in team with my employees, the hospital director and the patient organization.

**Personal Added Value, Examples** From discussions with my key clinical people, it was evident that we needed to expand our clinical services. There was need for establishing two new programs, one for adult patients with congenital heart disease and one for patients with heart disease caused by toxic side effects of cancer therapy. We had been aware of the needs of these increasing groups for several years, but for different reasons, we had not been able to establish adequate systems to take care of these patients. Based upon advice from my management group, I decided to establish two new programs to take better care of these patients. My defined objectives and personal added value would be to provide funding and to recruit competent doctors and nurses to do the job.

Our patients with congenital heart disease were taken well care of as children, but were often lost to follow up in their adult life. That was a threat to their health, as the patient organization appropriately and repeatedly pointed out.

To get the solutions we needed for patients with congenital heart disease, I needed to involve the patient organization since they had expertise which was essential for deciding what good service was. This was a pleasure since they knew exactly what was needed, they were well organized and could help me by putting pressure on the government to provide funding. After a few years work we were able to establish a service for this group of patients. We recruited and trained a team of excellent doctors and nurses.

The other patient group was cancer survivors, who often developed heart disease as early or late complications to cancer therapy. They were often not followed up adequately by medical specialists.

It was of great help that our hospital director, who was a previous oncologist, supported the program. He also advised me to travel to the MD Andersen Cancer Center in Houston, which is a leading cancer hospital, to learn about best practice. After my visit to this center, we knew what we needed to do, and thanks to funding from the hospital director and a donation from the local cancer foundation, we quickly established a service to take care of patients with cardiovascular complications after cancer therapy.

Importantly, the people who deserved to shine after these two objectives were reached, were the doctors and nurses who did the job, but also the patient organization and external people giving their time and funding to help. My personal added value was to set the objectives and make sure that things happened.

## 7.7     Do Employee Pulse Surveys

Some hospitals do annual employee pulse surveys. A culture of asking for employee feedback creates happier, more engaged employees, which in turn, has positive effects on hospital culture. Engaged employees are more productive and take less time off.

Employee surveys are tools in the format of annual or more frequent anonymous questionnaires distributed to all employees to measure engagement, morale, and working conditions and is a way to get direct feedback on leadership. Surveys may be effective provided they are well-designed and effectively administered, and are used to make changes. The surveys may serve as an indicator of organizational health as it pertains to personnel. The employee surveys may help to reveal organizational problems that need to be worked on and for the leader they may give some clues about his or her own areas for improvement.

# 8

# Useful Tips for Becoming a Better Leader

**Abstract** This chapter presents a number of tips which will be useful for all leaders.

## 8.1 Do You Really Need an MBA?

Having a master degree in business administration (MBA) or in health administration (MHA) is always useful for clinical leaders. Most of the clinical leaders I have employed, however, did not have an MBA or MHA, but got formal training in management after they were employed. They attended management courses organized by the hospital, and some took a course at the university. They did usually very well without a full academic degree in management.

I did an MHA prior to my first position as leader, and it was useful to know the fundamentals of management. My positive experience with the MHA was to a large extent due to the inspiring personality of Professor Ole T. Berg, who was Head of the institute, and my main teacher during the course at the Institute of Health and Society, University of Oslo. The institute specialized in training leaders in health care, and had an excellent program for master's studies.

O. A. Smiseth, *Managing a Hospital*, Business Guides on the Go,
https://doi.org/10.1007/978-3-031-17611-1_8

If you are a young health worker and consider a career as hospital leader, get formal management training without too much delay. Be ready to step in when opportunities suddenly are there, and they may come when you least expect it.

## 8.2    Does the Leader Need Medical Insight?

Since hospitals are knowledge-intensive organizations, it is always an advantage if leaders have some medical insight. For a hospital director (CEO), however, political skills may be as important as medical insights, and therefore being a medical doctor or qualified nurse becomes less important.

For heads of clinical departments or divisions, limited medical insight can be compensated by having good advisors, but this tends to increase bureaucracy. Importantly, when a nurse is leader of a clinical department or division, it is essential that she has a respected medical doctor in her team as medical advisor. On the other hand, one should not employ medical doctors as clinical leaders unless they are dedicated to take full responsibility as leaders and invest the time needed to do the "non-medical" part of the job.

## 8.3    Improve Your Weak Points

All leaders have weak points and should work continuously to improve their performance. Every year, pick at least a couple of weak points where you want to improve your performance. If you have a recent employee pulse survey where the employees were asked to express their opinion about the leader, there may be ideas for where you should improve.

## 8.4    Never Punish Collectively

Never punish a whole group collectively since that will be felt unfair and is very ineffective as feedback. Avoid giving single persons critique when others are watching, always do it under four eyes. You can praise an employee when others are watching. It may increase the effect, but do not do it repeatedly for the same person since the others in the team may feel it unfair that they do not get the same attention.

Critique should be given quickly and directly, and there should be a good explanation.

## 8.5 When Employees Do Serious Errors

When employees do serious errors in patient management, start with supporting them. Find out if the problem is a system weakness which it often is. When it is not a system error, try by all means to help the employee to improve skills. When you have decided there is no room for improvement, try a "nice exit" which means helping the person out of the organization. Sometimes offering to pay for an educational course is a nice end of the job since the employee then can have a chance of starting over again somewhere else and not losing too much face.

## 8.6 Don't Waste Time Checking Every Travel Bill

The leader has to approve travel bills, course expenses, costs of a summer party and expenses to other activities. The approval is usually done electronically by looking through the reimbursement form with a number of attachments for documentation. Do not waste your time with looking through these in detail. You just accept or if you suspect there may be a bad culture, you may delegate to your secretary to look through details before you accept. To help the employee avoid doing errors, let the reimbursement have a link to rules for travel bills and course expenses, so that everybody knows what is correct. In addition, every now and then, let your administrative staff do a point audit to see that things are in line with the rules. Adding an extra night at a hotel or adding kilometers to the travel distance is fraud and should have consequences for the employee.

## 8.7    How to Dress

The way you should dress depends on the culture and tradition at your workplace. Make sure you are always clean. Do not wear the most colorful or trendy clothes in the hospital. You are there for the patients and your employees, not to impress people of how good you look. Other than that, it is difficult to give general advice.

## 8.8    Be Friendly, But Not a Friend

If you are a friend with one of your subordinates you may be tempted to give that person preferences or his colleagues may accuse you of that. Therefore, being friend with any of your subordinates can lead to problems for yourself and the hospital.

## 8.9    Make Your Boss Shine

Do not talk negatively about your boss. This will lead to your subordinates talking negatively about you, and a bad culture develops.

It is your duty to give feedback to your boss so that he functions well. This is part of loyalty. It should not be too often and of course should be done in a one-on-one conversation.

Tell your boss when he is about to do a mistake. This is part of shared responsibility and is an important criterion of a healthy organizational culture. You are responsible for results in the unit where you are the boss, but part of your responsibility is to give feedback to your own boss when he is about to do a bad mistake. It is dangerous with leaders who have blind loyalty to their superior. It was well stated by Confucius; "He who flatters a man is his enemy. he who tells him of his faults is his maker."

## 8.10   Minimize Bureaucracy

In most hospitals in my country, there are five or more organizational levels with boards and directors between the "real chief" which is the minister of health, and the first working medical doctor. This means that along this line of command, information can be accidentally or intentionally filtered several times on its way down, or when important advice is flowing upstream to the minister of health.

It is difficult to see any advantages with such comprehensive bureaucracy. It weakens the command line and tends to give more power to lobbyists.

A disadvantage with layers of administrative people is that they are usually far away from the clinical units and that makes it difficult to understand what is going on when they get reports about problems like unacceptably long waiting times, financial deficits or other issues. At each of the several layers in the organization, there is staff, often very clever previous health workers. When they do not understand, it is tempting for this staff to send out requests for detailed reports from the hospitals. Their good intentions are too be of help, but that is not always the case.

What the medical people really hate is getting requests from the bureaucrats and staff to "do jobs for them" such as responding to questionnaires, giving comments to reports or reporting data.

> It is not uncommon that clinical leaders feel they are serving the administration and not the other way around.

## 8.11   Open-Plan Office: A Health Hazard?

If considering open-plan office, it is important to take into account the need for employees to find time to concentrate. This is important when doctors and nurses make preparations for their next patient, when summarizing complex data in a discharge note, and reading literature to make sure a patient receives correct medicine. Furthermore, when you make telephone calls to patients or discuss cases with a colleague, it is not consistent with laws and regulations on confidentiality that someone who by chance happen to be in the same room can listen. A solution with a couple of nearby "quiet rooms" is useful.

It is argued that open office increases the risk of sick leave due to more stress and more virus infections. The jury is still out on this issue.

## 8.12 Negativity Is Like a Contagious Disease: Stop It

In any organization, there are people who enjoy more speaking about the negative than the positive, often finding people with similar attitude at lunch time. This tends to become a bad habit which can weaken the organization. In many cases, the reason behind the negativity is frustration for matters inside or outside the job. The leader of the person should address the problem during the regular leader–employee talk.

Constructive criticism is different and is needed as part of the improvement process. When hiring people, ask the references about attitudes, including how the applicant contributes to a good work environment.

## 8.13 Loyalty Is as Fundamental as Honesty

When something has been decided by your superior and you are going to implement, do not say "the boss has decided and therefore we have to ….." As a leader, you should own the decision yourself, and express this to the employees as your decision.

It is important to express your opinion to your boss when you disagree, and a good boss will incorporate your feedback in his decision. To express your opinion and criticize a decision before it is final, is an important part of loyalty. When you disagree on major issues after having given feedback to your boss several times, and you still disagree, it may be time to consider stepping down from your position.

## 8.14 The Right Attitude

A leader of course should have the attitude of an employer and not of the employee. When this fails, there is a severe management problem. I sometimes get requests from head hunters regarding persons who are candidates for leadership positions. When I give them my advice, there is one qualification which excludes from becoming a good leader, and that is disloyalty.

In management, attitude separates wheat from chaff.

## 8.15 Managing Prima Donnas

If a prima donna weakens the team, he should change behavior or have to leave. Offer a stepwise program with couching. They often have support from a number of colleagues and this complicates the process. It is even more complicated if the patients send you support letters for the prima donna. There is no easy solution, but make sure that your clinical leaders as well as your superior supports your decision.

## 8.16 In-hospital Romance and Forbidden Love

Dating between employees is inevitable and often ends in happy marriages. But still romances at work are challenging for both leaders and employees. In the UK, more than 70% of the employees have experienced a romance at work (Clarke, 2006). According to a more recent survey from the USA produced by the job site Vault and discussed by Dr. Kim Elsesser (2019), 72% of those over 50 years had been romantically involved with a co-worker. As Dr. Elsesser commented, there was concern with attitudes revealed in this report, as almost three in four would participate in a workplace romance again if given the chance.

'Date and tell' rather than strict prohibition.

There is no legal obligation for the employees to inform their leader that they have an in-hospital romance. Perhaps due to fear of violating human rights, relatively few organizations have a formal romance policy (Wilson, 2015).

If a company wants to have official company rules, one option is a 'date and tell' strategy, which implies that the couple informs their leaders or HR manager, and one of the involved gets another position in the company (Clarke, 2006). For a "date and tell" strategy to work the rules must be communicated to the employees as part of the company's sexual harassment policy.

In contrast to romances outside the workplace, which may end without external noise, a workplace romance may degenerate into accusations of sexual harassment. Having a relationship with a superior can lead to rumors that your professional success is due to a sexual relationship with your boss. Figure 8.1 illustrates examples of problematic relations.

Hierarchical romances are most problematic.

## Not acceptable relations at work

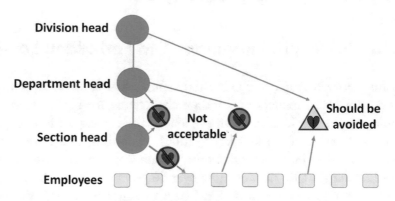

**Fig. 8.1** Problematic workplace romances: Dating should not occur unless there are more than two organizational levels between the couple. Furthermore, it is considered inappropriate for a high-level manager to date someone much lower in the organization. Copyright: Otto A. Smiseth

Workplace romances are classified as either lateral, when the couple are at the same level in the organization, and hierarchical when a manager is romantically involved with a subordinate. Hierarchical workplace romances are both most frequent and most problematic as they involve power differences (Powell, 2001). In some cases, a leader may have an ego motive and the lower-rank employee a job-related motive (i.e., one participant satisfies sexual needs in exchange for the other participant satisfying desire for promotion or other career-related needs) (Powell & Foley, 1998). Importantly, a relationship between people who are not managers is usually no real problem.

It is generally accepted to forbid this dating:

– Between supervisor and individual in same line of command, unless there is more than two organizational levels between.
– Between two leaders who report to the same boss.

## 8.17  Avoid Nepotism

Preferential appointment of family members is named nepotism, a term which originates from the Catholic Church, where it was common practice in ancient times that popes and bishops assigned their *nephews* to important positions in the church.

It is considered inappropriate, and in some states and countries, it is illegal to appoint family members to positions within the organization. The problem is most severe for management positions. Giving relatives unfair employment opportunities or promotion to better-paid positions weakens morale within the company.

Some companies have strict regulations and prohibit spouses or relatives from working in the same company, but with the exception of relatives to the director (CEO), this may be considered too rigid. Importantly, no hospital or other company should allow family members or close friends to have positions within the same chain of authority or to be in the same management team which reports to the same boss. In some companies, a relationship is acceptable when there are more than two organizational levels between the two family members. These principles

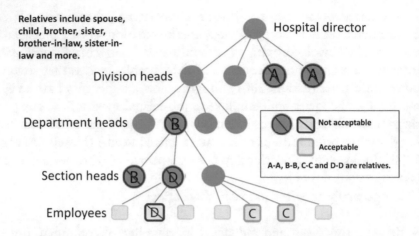

**Fig. 8.2** Nepotism: Schematic illustrations showing examples of positions which are not acceptable or acceptable for family or close friends. In this regard, family means individuals related within two degrees by blood or marriage and includes in-laws. AA means two persons are relatives, and the same for BB, CC and DD. Copyright: Otto A. Smiseth

are illustrated in Fig. 8.2. However, even with two or three levels between there may be problems, and therefore this should ideally be avoided. In smaller family-owned companies, the rules are different.

The following case illustrates that nepotism can be a problem even when there are several layers between family members.

**Nepotism Case**  At one of the hospitals in a central part of Europe, there were several applicants for position as leader of a department which specialized in esophageal surgery. The position was given to a candidate who was married to the chief of the larger hospital cluster. A complaint was filed from one of the competitors for the position. The HR manager responded that this relationship did not matter since there were three levels of leaders between this applicant and her husband on the top. Therefore, this was in keeping with the rule at the hospital which was that there should be more than two organizational levels between family members when working as leaders.

A couple of years later, it was obvious that the chief of the hospital cluster was about to make unfair decisions to secure the department of his wife more patients. The result would be that two other hospitals in the cluster under his jurisdiction would suffer from loss of patients to a degree that threatened the quality of their surgery. Fortunately, this misuse of power was observed, and the initiative was stopped.

The lesson from this case is that nepotism may be a problem when family members are leaders at several levels in the line of command.

For people working in non-management jobs, it is usually no problem that family members are in the same company. Furthermore, in many small towns, the hospital is one of the largest employers and then it would be unreasonable to be very strict on these rules.

## 8.18   #meetoo

Every hospital is committed to providing a workplace that is free from sexual harassment. Such behavior in a workplace is against the law and shall not be tolerated. When the hospital determines that an allegation of sexual harassment is credible, it must take prompt and appropriate corrective action.

When an employee complains that she or he is experiencing sexual harassment of any type, the employer has an obligation to investigate the charges thoroughly. The employer cannot decide whether to believe the employee, but must start by assuming that allegations are correct.

Every hospital should have a procedure to handle cases with sexual harassment and every leader should have a course on the topic so that they know how to work with prevention and how to act when they get a case. When it occurs, it is important to seek advice and help from the HR-unit. Furthermore, it is very important to follow the procedure in the hospital for handling such problems.

## 8.19   Zero-Tolerance for Harassment

Every large organization may occasionally have employees with a behavior which is outside the accepted norm. Such people should quickly get feedback from their superior. If the problem continues, and in particular if there is persistent harassment directed towards single employees or groups of employees, the HR manager should look into the issue to find solutions. Since this kind of problems often has lasted for a long time, the leader may have developed negative attitudes towards the alleged problematic employee, and therefore it could be good to have an unbiased evaluation of the situation. Most large hospitals have people with competence in handling problems that relate to work environment, who can investigate the issue and propose measures to be undertaken. The ownership to the problem should all the time be with the leader. In some cases, the problematic employee will be dismissed.

## 8.20    Show Respect for the Non-medical Personnel

For a leader as well as for the medical and nursing staff, it is important to show respect for people who work with non-medical tasks. This can be small things as saying hello and talking to the individuals when you meet in the hallway.

## 8.21    Hiring and Dismissing People

There is often a few months trial time for new employees, and during this time, it must be determined if the contract is permanent. In most state- or government-owned hospitals it is very difficult to dismiss people even when their performance is way below standards. Therefore, it is critically important to employ the right people, and in particular when it comes to recruiting leaders.

When employing new leaders, you should follow the two levels up rule, also named the grandmother or grandfather principle. This means you have to consult the leader one level above yourself and get acceptance before you can employ a new leader below yourself.

When seeking advice on whom to employ, never trust only the last employer since he may have reasons to get rid of the person. Try to get advice from the next last employer. Furthermore, avoid taking advice from friends of the candidate.

When building teams, remember that A-leaders like to recruit A-employees, whereas B-leaders tend to recruit C-employees.

If you have too many low performers in an organization, it is very difficult to create a healthy culture even with a couple of excellent leaders on the top of the organization. Mediocracy is like a chronic infection and is very hard to cure.

If a person is a low performer with no realistic potential for improvement in your department, it is very important to be quick and terminate the contract. Make sure that HR helps you with doing everything correct and according to laws and regulations. Equally important is to treat the person with respect, be pleasant and explain well the reasons why he should not continue. You may also consider to give the employee a nice exit by giving a few months stipend to study something which may be useful for future job applications.

## 8.22 Don't Let the HR People Pick Leaders

The most important decisions you make is selection of leaders. You are personally responsible for the results of your unit, and it is critical that you are the one who selects your subordinate leaders. Do not let the HR people make the choice. The main role of the HR people is to help you with sticking to rules for employment. Let the HR manager check that diplomas and degrees are from universities which you trust and that the person really completed the degree.

The HR leader should not decide which salary should be offered. She only advises you and you decide.

## 8.23 Support Employees When They Need You

Occasionally, there are people in the system with a problem mentally or physically, and therefore do not have potential to work as expected. I think every hospital should have room for a few people who cannot work like the others. I consider this as part of the social responsibility of every large or even small company.

Sometimes an employee has a personal or family problem which needs attention. It could be because a child has a problem and needs one of the parents to spend more time at home. It is good for the employee and for the organization that we are flexible, and accept to change the work schedule when there is a good reason to do so.

Depressions are relatively common as a reaction to things happening in life or as an endogenic disorder. Depressed people may have reduced energy and cannot go full speed. It is often difficult to know when people are depressed, but in some cases, it is obvious. This should be respected, and importantly, show empathy whenever you are in contact with somebody who is a low performer for such reasons.

## 8.24 Do Not Allow Administrative Staff Mess Up the Command Line

Always remember that the administrative staff are advisors and not line leaders. When you run your regular management group meetings with the department heads and key administrative staff (HR manager and finance manager), a good rule is that essentially all communication should be between you and the department heads. The staff should not interfere, but only talk when you want them to. Sometimes you want them to have a presentation and that is fine. It may happen, however, that the administrative staff takes over the meeting, and the department heads are allowed very comfortably to abdicate. The staff tends to enjoy this interaction, but it ruins the command line and the impact of the meeting.

## 8.25    When You Need a Good Lawyer

If you are in a tough situation and need a lawyer, go outside and get the best in town. Lawyers in hospital are just fine for managing routine administrative issues, but tend to become too far from real life to help you when you have tough cases. When your opponent has hired top lawyers, you need to match this with someone at the same level.

For a hospital to employ its own team of top lawyers will be more expensive than hiring from the outside a few times when you have tough issues.

## 8.26    When the Leader Takes It All

A few years ago, I was attending a large medical conference in the USA and a key note lecture was delivered by one of the most famous experts in the field, who was also leader of a clinical department. The expert gave a great lecture on how to do mini-invasive heart valve surgery. The large room was packed with people. At the end of the lecture, it was time for asking questions. A middle-aged man raised from his seat and moved quickly to the microphone. The question to the speaker was "how many of these surgeries have you done yourself?" The speaker gave a vague answer. Then the man asked again, and again, each time a bit more aggressive. Apparently, an internal conflict was brought on stage, and the chairman of the session took action, by concluding that the session had ended, and it was time for lunch.

It was obvious for everybody that the "expert" had never done the surgery he was talking about, whereas the man who asked the questions was the one who had done the surgeries. The experience was embarrassing to everybody in the room.

The lesson from this case is that you should always credit the people who did the job. When the leader takes all the credit, some people get badly hurt, and in their eyes, the image of the leader falls like a stone.

# References

Clarke, L. (2006). Sexual relationships and sexual conduct in the workplace. *Legal Studies, 26*, 347–368.

Elsesser, K. (2019). *These 6 surprising office romance stats should be a wake-up call for organizations.* https://www.forbes.com/sites/kimelsesser/2019/02/14/these-6-surprising-office-romance-stats-should-be-a-wake-up-call-to-organizations/#4014c8a923a2

Powell, G. N. (2001). Workplace romances between senior-level executives and lower-level employees: An issue of work disruption and gender. *Human Relations (New York), 54*(11), 1519–1544.

Powell, G. N., & Foley, S. (1998). Something to talk about: Romantic relationships in organizational settings. *Journal of Management, 24 (3)*, 421–448.

Wilson, F. (2015). Romantic relationships at work: Why love can hurt. *International Journal of Management Reviews, 17*, 1–19.

# 9

# How to Meet the Press

**Abstract** If you are contacted by a journalist about a sensitive issue, consult the hospital press office to discuss how to respond. Never have more than two points you would like to make, preferably just one. If you have too many points, nothing will sink in.

Never go into an interview with a journalist unless you have a clear message. Do not see the journalist as an enemy, but as a means to get your message through to an audience.

If you are on direct TV and you feel pressed into a corner, take the lead. Stay more ruthlessly with your key message, but be calm and friendly and remember to smile.

After a bad clinical incident, and you are on TV to explain what went wrong, always start with expressing your sympathy with the patient and the patient's family. Never start with being defensive. As the leader, you are responsible for everything done in your unit, including all the errors.

When you apologize, make it personal. Do not say things like "it is regrettable," "the hospital is sorry for what happened" or similar. Make it personal and say "I apologize for what happened, and I am very sorry for this."

# 9.1    The art of Communication with Media

The journalists are professional, while you are probably an amateur in communication. Follow some ground rules.

If you are contacted by a journalist about a sensitive issue, consult the press office at your hospital to discuss how to respond. Before accepting to give an interview, always demand to approve the final version of what will be printed in the media. In case a TV interview is planned, rehearse with your media people on expected difficult questions.

You should know the mathematics of communication which is shown graphically in Fig. 9.1. One multiplied by one equals one, and two multiplied by one equals two. However, 6 multiplied by one equals zero because with so many messages, nothing will be remembered. Never have more than 2 points you would like to make, preferably just one. If you have too many points, nothing will sink in.

# 9.2    Be Prepared for Media Scandals

You must never go into an interview with a journalist unless you have a clear message. Never accept door stepping, which may force you to give an unprepared interview.

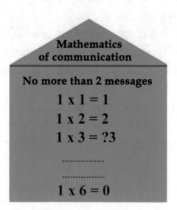

**Fig. 9.1**    The mathematics of communication: Try to have just one message, start with it and conclude with it. Copyright: Otto A. Smiseth

If you get a telephone from the media, do not answer any questions right away, but tell you will contact the journalist after you have received an e-mail about what is the issue. The journalist probably is recording the conversation, and therefore be careful that you answer friendly and politely. One time I received a telephone Friday at 6.30 pm, when arriving at home after a long day at work, and ready to enjoy the beef which I could hear frying in the pan. There was a journalist on the phone, and she wanted to know if I had given a high-level health politician privileges, which were unfair. The dinner was ready, and I decided to get the conversation done quickly so that I could enjoy the dinner. My brief and stressful conversation was later that evening played as part of prime-time news on national TV. It sounded as if I and the hospital had a problem. It later turned out that one of the employees for unknown reasons, had misinformed the journalist. For me this was anyway a bad incident which happened because I did not follow the golden rule which is to stay calm, and say you will call back.

Before you meet media, talk to the press office of your hospital. They can help you, and importantly, protect you from doing something which is not smart. Always have somebody else, including the media people, read through your written statements. Always request that the journalist sends you the final text for approval before it is published. Usually they will, but the ingress (opening paragraph) they will not let you see, and you have to accept this way of doing it. If they want photos of you and come with a photographer, take control of the photo scenes and limit the number of photos. If they take multiple photos in different situations, they may use some really bad ones which shows you with awkward expressions.

In difficult cases, make a position card with help from the hospital press office, before you meet the press. Make a briefing note with a set of messages.

Do not see the journalist as an enemy, but as a means to get your message through to an audience. Do not act as if the journalist is your audience, she is just a transmitter. You should speak as if you communicate directly with the people who will watch the TV or read the newspaper.

Remember, the journalist needs a story. Have a story ready—make it simple for the journalist.

Do not introduce anything negative. Do not repeat negative statements, rather say "I disagree." Avoid saying yes or no. Do not say "no comment," instead explain briefly why you cannot comment.

When there is a media case that involves your unit, always inform the press office in the hospital. When media calls, you may tell them to call the press office.

In principle, every leader can answer the press regarding general medical issue within their own responsibility, but not when the issue is about politics, economy, or other questions which relate to hospital management. Then the hospital management should take over.

## 9.3    Tips and Pitfalls During TV Interview

Sit quietly back in the chair with open shoulders at start and end of the interview. Do not stand up right after the interview. Sit quiet for some seconds.

If you are recorded on video and you are not happy with a statement, stop the sequence and start over again.

Look at the journalist (focus between her eyes) during the interview. Do not look into the camera.

If you are on direct TV and the interviewer makes things difficult, and you feel you are pressed into a corner, take the lead, like the rugby player who takes the ball and runs with it. Stay more ruthlessly with your key message. Zoom in and give examples, then zoom out and talk in general, but always get back to your key message. Stay calm, friendly and decisive and remember to smile.

## 9.4    The Art of Apologizing

After a bad incident with a patient, and you have to explain on TV what went wrong, always start with expressing your sympathy with the patient and the patient's family. Make it personal, say that you are sorry and your body language should express that. This applies even when you and the hospital have done nothing wrong. Then slowly explain why things went wrong. Never start with being defensive.

Remember, as the leader, you are responsible for everything done in your unit, including all the errors. If there has been a bad event like an unexpected complication during surgery, you are as a leader always personally responsible, unless it is obvious otherwise or an investigation has concluded differently.

When you apologize, make sure it is personal. Do not say things like "it is regrettable," "the hospital is sorry for what happened" or similar. Make it personal and say "I apologize for what happened, and I am very sorry for this." In the media, do not blame your employees since that looks bad from the patient perspective and is disloyal towards your employees. After you have personally apologized, you may explain what happened, and that measures will be taken to make sure it will never happen again.

# 10

# How to Get Control Over Your Own Time?

**Abstract** The following strategies will make you more efficient: (1) Structure your meeting plan according to Sect. 4.4, (2) optimize e-mail handling, (3) get rid of the monkey, and (4) delegate as much as you can.

Over-checking mails is a major source of inefficiency. There is usually no need to respond instantly. Avoid a crowded inbox, which makes you read the mails over again each time you open the mailbox. Archiving emails into many different folders, wastes lots of time. Consider to give your secretary access to your mailbox, and she can handle "unimportant" mails for you.

Monkeys on the back is a metaphor of reverse delegation, where employees overload you with problems they should have solved themselves. *Have a friendly talk with the subordinates to get* things right with regard to expectations, and understanding who is working for whom.

For delegation to work, follow the basic rules. First, make sure that the person who gets the task has competence to do it. Second, give direction, but do not say how to do the job. Third, have a plan for checking that the job is done. If the latter is not taken care of, you have not delegated, but abdicated.

O. A. Smiseth, *Managing a Hospital*, Business Guides on the Go,
https://doi.org/10.1007/978-3-031-17611-1_10

The following methods and strategies will help you take back and maintain control over your own time. They will help you to get home from work before the kids go to bed, and will give you time for recreation and other activities in the weekend.

1. Make sure your meeting plan is efficient. This is addressed in Sects. 4.4 and 4.5.
2. Optimize e-mail handling.
3. Get rid of the monkey.
4. Delegate as much as you can, and do it right.

## 10.1    Optimize e-Mail Handling

There is a significant amount of research on what is smart and efficient handling of e-mails (Plummer, 2019). What is efficient, depends on preferences, and may also depend on expectations and traditions in your organization. There are, however, a few obvious sources of inefficiency and some of them are discussed in this chapter.

Over-checking mails is a major source of inefficiency. This is because mail checking distracts you, and it takes a significant time to get back to continue the work you were doing. In most cases, there is no need to respond instantly to the mails.

Avoid having a crowded inbox which makes you read the mails over again each time you open the mailbox.

Archiving emails into many different folders using a mouse, wastes lots of time. It is recommended to have just a couple of folders for archiving, including one for mails you need to follow up on. If you have many folders, you spend time both on deciding where to move the mail and on the operation with the mouse to move the mail to the selected folders.

Current mail systems have excellent search tools, which are much faster than looking through a list of mail folders. You probably already use it when you look for mails in your Sent Mails folder, and find it works very well. Don't let habits from the early days of e-mailing slow you down.

Reading and processing irrelevant mail is another waste of time and can be easily managed by setting suitable filters.

Do not use your job mail for private correspondence. There are many examples on how this can give trouble for either you or your employer.

Avoid that your subordinates send you lots of mails which occupies your time. In general, when I send a mail to someone to help me respond to a "trivial" request from the hospital administration or someone else, I do not want mails back from them. I expect that they just do the job. The exception of course, is when there is something I need to follow up.

You should clean up the content in a mail before you forward it. Having a long history of correspondence which is hanging on, is common, but is a waste for the recipient who may think he needs to read it all. Delete all the "garbage" before you respond or forward an e-mail.

If one of your subordinates bother you with too many mails and you are fortunate to have a good secretary, you can give her access to your mailbox, and she can handle these mails for you. Reducing back-and-forth mails is a big time saver.

Your e-mail manners impact not only your life, but also affects the efficiency of other members of your team. Figure 10.1 summarizes what may be considered bad manners when it comes to e-mails.

**Bad e-mail manners – to be avoided**

✓ Send no job mails during the weekend

✓ Never send nasty mails

✓ Do not bother people with many attachments

✓ Do not send copy to «everybody»

✓ Avoid sending trivial mail to a busy leader

**Fig. 10.1** Bad e-mail manners—to be avoided. Copyright Otto A. Smiseth

## 10.2    Get Rid of the Monkey

In a Harvard Business Review article, Oncken and Wass (1974) presented a fascinating analysis of why leaders typically run out of time because they accumulate problems which belong to and should be resolved by their subordinate leaders. As a metaphor of problems that subordinate leaders cannot resolve themselves, they use monkeys.

When a subordinate leader has a problem, he may seek help from his boss. If the boss cannot answer right away, he may respond that he will answer in a day or two. In this case, the subordinate leader has successfully moved the monkey from his own shoulder to the back of his boss. This means that the boss has accepted to provide a solution to a problem which primarily was not his problem, but the problem of his subordinate. If other subordinate leaders also are allowed to transfer monkeys to the back of the boss, things get even worse. If the problems are not resolved when weekend arrives, the boss will spend time caring for and feeding the monkeys, whereas the subordinate leaders can enjoy a nice weekend in the sun (Fig. 10.2). This is named reverse delegation.

During lunch on the following Monday, the employees complain about their leader as a person who cannot make decisions.

*The problem of reverse delegation* is relevant for most leaders and limits their time and ability to execute their job as a leader. If you have received too many monkeys on your shoulder and spend most of the time feeding them, you *become a bottle neck in the organization.*

One year the employee survey from my management group gave me negative ratings in two categories. First, I was not available enough and did to resolve problems as well as they expected. Initially the results made me a little disappointed, before I suddenly realized that this was a great opportunity for getting things right with regard to expectations from my subordinates and understanding who is working for whom. I had a nice talk with my management group about my expectations to them according to the philosophy of keeping the monkey on the appropriate shoulder. If they did what they were supposed to do, I would have more time available for them. Furthermore, I explained that since they preferred using one or two days a week to do clinical work or research, they had

**Fig. 10.2** The problem of reverse delegation using monkey as metaphor: A boss (left side of figure) who accumulates problems which his subordinate leader (right side) should have resolved himself. Copyright: Otto A. Smiseth

enough flexible time which could be used to fulfill their job as leaders, whereas I was overbooked with work as their leader. Therefore, they had plenty of time to do the tasks which they tended to put on my shoulder.

# 10.3 Delegate as Much as You Can, But Do It Right

Delegation makes you more efficient and your subordinates grow personally from the joy of getting more senior tasks and by the faith you show them. Importantly, you can delegate the task, but not the responsibility.

For delegation to work, there are some basic rules. First, do not delegate unless the person who gets the task has competence and training to do it. Second, give direction, but do not say how you want the job done. Third, have a plan for following up that the job is done. If the latter is not taken care of, you have not delegated, but abdicated.

You may need to customize how you delegate. Some employees do blindly what you tell. They are risky since they may forget process with employees. In particular, if you are a quick fixer and the one you delegate to, is also a quick fixer, there can be some dangerous synergy. At the other extreme, there are employees who repeatedly come back to you to ask what to do and check if you agree. Then the delegation is the opposite of a time saver. The ideal subordinate is the one who quickly understands, but comes back to you for discussion when there are important challenges.

If what you really want is to have somebody look into a case and bring it back to you so that you can make a good decision, this is not delegation. Then you have transferred the task to a case worker, which is often useful, but is not delegation. When you delegate, you give another person authority to decide on your behalf.

**A Real-Life Case of Severe Delegation Failure** A few years ago, in a small hospital in Europe, things went completely wrong due to delegation failure. This hospital had problems with keeping appropriate waiting times for patients referred for suspected cancer. The hospital director blamed this on budgetary limitations. He did not want to transfer the patients to other hospitals, however, since that would lead to further cuts in the hospital budget.

Because all physicians were overbooked, many patients had to wait several months to get their cancer diagnosis verified or excluded. The medical doctors informed the director of this critical capacity problem. The doctors were not motivated to spend more time on administration of waiting lists. They would rather use their limited time to work directly with patients. Rather than hiring more doctors, the hospital director decided to delegate to his secretaries to find vacant spots for the patients who were referred for suspected cancer.

There were some tragic events of cancer progression due to delayed diagnostics.

Ultimately, complaints from patients were brought to the media, and the health authorities took action. The director was fired for his negligence.

The secretaries were not to blame since they did their best, but were not trained for the specific task, which was to prioritize among different potential cancer patients.

When considering this case from the outside, it is obvious that the hospital director did two severe delegation errors. First, he did not make sure that those who were delegated the task had the competence and training needed to do it properly. Second, he did not follow up that the patients were taken care of. He in fact abdicated, which was dangerous since then, nobody took responsibility for the cancer patients who were forgotten in the hospital database. For a hospital director, the primary obligation is to have systems in place which take care of patients.

# References

Oncken, Jr., W., & Wass, D. L. (1974). Management time: Who's got the monkey? *Harvard Business Review*, November–December.
Plummer, M. (2019). How to spend way less time on email every day. *Harvard Business Review*, January 22.

# Glossary

**Administrative staff;** Includes human resources (HR) managers, finance managers and patient safety officers.

**CEO;** Central executive officer, meaning the highest ranked leader in the organization. Most places in this book the title Hospital Director is used instead of CEO.

**CT;** Computed tomography.

**Department;** In this book, department is the organizational structure under the divisions. Therefore, the department head reports to the division head. In some countries it is the other way around with departments as the largest organizational structure.

**Division;** The organizational structure immediately below the hospital director. In some countries division means smaller units further down in the organization.

**EHS;** Environmental Health and Safety.

**HR manager;** Human resources manager.

**MRI;** Magnetic resonance imaging.

**Outcome;** Health outcome is change in health after treatment. Includes different measures of morbidity, mortality and complications to procedures.

O. A. Smiseth, *Managing a Hospital*, Business Guides on the Go,
https://doi.org/10.1007/978-3-031-17611-1

**PET;** Positron emission tomography

**Section;** In this book, section means smaller units within a department.

**Support staff;** People working as secretaries and with information technology, maintenance, cleaning, patient transport and other basic functions.

Printed in the United States
by Baker & Taylor Publisher Services